We Got Issues!

Inner Ocean Publishing, Inc.
P.O. Box 1239
Makawao, Maui, HI 96768-1239
www.innerocean.com

Cover and book design by Design Action Collective
Julia Ahumada Grob, Editorial Assistant
Alli Maxwell, Research Assistant

Inner Ocean Publishing is a member of Green Press Initiative, a nonprofit program
dedicated to supporting publishers in their efforts to reduce their use of fiber sourced
from endangered forests. We elected to print this title on 50% postconsumer recycled
paper with the recycled portion processed chlorine free. As a result, we have saved
the following resources: 218 trees, 10,192 lbs of solid waste, 79,366 gallons of water,
19,121 lbs of net greenhouse gases, 152 million BTU's. For more information on the
Green Press Initiative, visit http://www.greenpressinitiative.org.

We got issues! : a young woman's guide to a bold, courageous and empowered life /
Rha Goddess & JLove Calderón. -- Maui, Hawaii : Inner Ocean Publishing, 2006.
p. ; cm.
ISBN-13: 978-1-930722-72-9 (pbk.)
ISBN-10: 1-930722-72-9 (pbk.)

1. Women--Social conditions--Literary collections. 2. Feminism--Literary collections.
3. Women--Identity. 4. Feminist literature.
I. Rha Goddess. II. Calderón, Jennifer.
HQ1155 .W44 2006 305.42--dc22   0610

TK

Printed in the United States of America
05 06 07 08 09 10 DATA 10 9 8 7 6 5 4 3 2 1

DISTRIBUTED BY PUBLISHER'S GROUP WEST
For information on promotions, bulk purchases, premiums, or educational use, please
contact: 866.731.2216 or sales@innerocean.com.

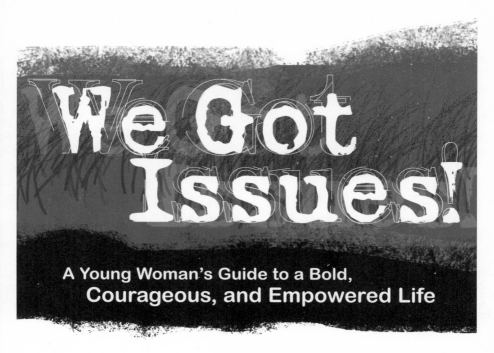

We Got Issues!

A Young Woman's Guide to a Bold, Courageous, and Empowered Life

Rha Goddess & JLove Calderón, Editors

INNER OCEAN PUBLISHING

Maui • San Francisco

To the legacy of bold, courageous, and empowered women . . .

Incantation

by Sara Littlecrow Russell

It's not a voting box—
It's a cauldron
Ritual container
Object of power
Receptacle
For spells and prayers
Curses and dreams.

Let's gather together and brew some magik
Let's gather together and brew some ceremony
Let's gather together and brew some change

Mix the blood of an Iraqi child
With the sweat of a Bangladeshi factory worker
Add the ashes of a lay-off notice
And the venom of a congressional snake

Stir it well, sister,
Stir it well.

Add a pinch of uranium from the floor of a Navajo miner's kitchen
And a drop of potassium chloride from an execution chamber
But don't forget
The skin of a slave,
The scalp of a cavalry officer,
The finger of Chinese railroad worker.

Stir it well, sister,
Stir it well.

Let's make a charm or powerful trouble.
Sisters we need to make a fire that burns so hot
Our ballots burn through the sides of the voting box
So blend in the roar of a lioness
The bite of a wolf-bitch
The swat of a mother bear
The sting of a queen bee
Now . . . the ceremony is complete.

Contents

Introduction

Rha speaks:

In the spring of 2002, I was invited to give a keynote address at the first annual Women & Power summit at Omega Institute. That's when I began talking to all the young women in my life about the P word. Elizabeth Lesser, Omega's cofounder, wanted me to speak about the "next wave," where I thought young women were headed, and how they approached claiming, using, and having (or not having) power. In the many conversations that led up to and came out of the summit, I became acutely aware of both the crisis and opportunity facing young women in their quest for agency, influence, effectiveness, and recognition.

In August of the following year, I found myself totally uninspired by the frenzy of political mobilization. In response, I invited six of my closest artist-activist colleagues to come together and explore what young women's social and political power in the United States could be. Over the course of three days, we laughed, raged, cried, and envisioned a world where young women could be heard, where the passion of our words and the determination of our spirits would be felt by those who claim to represent the leadership of this nation. In a moment of raw honesty, we named this project We Got Issues!

Don't you?

Knowing that we weren't alone, *We Got Issues!* went on the road in the fall of 2003 to create a national dialogue among eighteen- to thirty-five-year-old women about electoral politics and our most crucial concerns as members of U.S. society. For more than twelve months, we traveled across the nation, reaching out to young women everywhere and asking them about their politics and their hearts.

Women in Ohio told us about a recent divorce, or being attacked on campus while walking to the dorm, or finally leaving behind the boyfriend who hurt way more than he loved.

We broke bread in the dining rooms and kitchens of women from Seattle to Brooklyn as they gathered for book clubs and brunches; we held "rantfest"-style open mics in churches and community centers. We sat in the grass with young women in Washington, D.C., when more than a million women gathered for the March for Women's Lives; we went to the National Hip-Hop Political Convention in New Jersey, where more than 150 women linked arms and cried for a young women who had lost her child, and applauded another who became a Hip-Hop poet-preacher.

We went to the women's penitentiary at Rikers Island, where we weren't allowed to bring pencils or pens to give to the girls for "safety reasons." Later, we couldn't write fast enough to record the pain, the innocence, the guilt, the suffocation, the loss of these forty-five young women sitting right in front of us, and the loss of their voices in our community "on the outside." That year of listening had a profound effect on us, as we celebrated the power of sisterhood and learned what our sisters wanted and needed in order to thrive.

JLove speaks:

As someone who has worked with young people for the past twelve years, I was excited to be supporting women my age. Our culture tells us that once you hit a certain age you're not allowed to need help anymore—you should have it figured out by now. But what if you haven't? What if I haven't? I myself was looking for development in that next-level shit. Yeah, I felt accomplished in certain areas— youth development, facilitating healing spaces for young women, youth and Hip-Hop activism—but I had hit my own ceiling of expertise. What's next for me? I often thought. We Got Issues! *helped me find what I was looking for, and it rocked my world from the inside out. Helping other women develop as leaders and transforming my own life on a new level felt so powerful bouncing around in my body that I needed a release, a physical sign of my complete shift. The day I couldn't hold it in anymore, I went short 'n' pink. My hair. I chopped off the brown hair that had cascaded down my back for so long, and I dyed what was left hot pink—'cause that had become the color of my soul.*

These conversations created an acute awareness of the painful silences and the critical need to celebrate the voices of our sisters everywhere. Our visions, songs, movements, and battle cries have the power to preserve, heal, and protect families, communities, and the globe. Yet all too often this power is hidden.

Rha speaks:

When we started, I just assumed that women would rush to the mic to participate. I had no idea just how much encouragement and affirmation young women would need in order to speak their minds authentically. Quiet as it's kept, young women in this country expect to be ignored. There's an unspoken assumption that we are here only to service the needs of others. Most young women believe that people don't really want to know what we think. My most powerful moments in this project have been watching young women move out of their silence and into their truths.

Watching women push against class, culture, personal fears, and years of abuse has taught me to never take my own voice for granted.

This project is not about who can speak the loudest or the most often. This project is about lifting the veil of silence that enshrouds all of us, in ways we don't even realize. It's about cracking the expertly made-up façade that most of us hide behind, to get real with ourselves and each other.

According to a recent report issued by the Annenberg Public Policy Center and a similar study conducted by the Center for American Women and Politics, even though women represent fifty-one percent of the general population in this country, we make up less than fifteen percent of the top professional executive, and political leadership. If we consider women of color, the statistics are three percent for political leadership and six percent professional leadership.

Yet here at WGI!, we know that young women are demonstrating leadership all the time. They share a great sense of passion about their lives, their families, and their communities. They are a significant majority of the nonprofit workforce, and volunteer twice as much as their male counterparts—and that's not even counting all of the unpaid care many of them provide to their extended families and communities. Young women are deeply concerned about the politics of safety, respect, education, gainful employment, faith, health, and community. But these contributions often go unacknowledged by the media, by our larger society, and sometimes even by the women who make them!

JLove speaks:

And then there's our celebrity-obsessed pop culture, which glamorizes Britney-style sexual display, casts women of color almost exclusively as video hos, and recognizes humanitarian work only when Angelina Jolie is doing it. These are just some of the reasons that we got issues.

We Got Issues! is a movement designed to tap into the transformative power of creative expression as a vehicle for awakening a new brand of feminine-centered leadership and social/political activism in America.

WGI! is committed to *all* young women age eighteen to thirty-five, especially those from the most marginalized communities: immigrants, indigenous people, people of color, the working poor, queer folks.

Rha speaks:

After collecting almost 1,000 voices, WGI! commissioned a team of amazing young female writers to create more than eighty monologues that became the core script for the WGI! Performance Piece. We searched among artist-activists, theatrical actors, community organizers, and everyday young women for the perfect cast to embody these voices. We wanted the range we'd encountered to be reflected not just in the words, but also in the physical presence of these women. When we identified our perfect ten, they all gathered in New York for a grueling six-week rehearsal process. Even though the days were long and challenging, these women took on the great responsibility they had been given.

On September 13, 2004, just fifty days before the 2004 presidential election, WGI! mounted our world premiere at the famous Apollo Theater in New York for a sold-out audience of more than 1,100 people. "Vaginas Rock, Chicks Vote" was executive produced by Eve Ensler, Jane Fonda, and the antiviolence organization V-Day, and featured famous actors, musicians, and political activists. WGI! opened the show and received a standing ovation. Our greatest accomplishment that night was the fulfillment of our mission to make the voices of young women who often fall between the cracks *heard*.

JLove speaks:

Collecting the rants was our pregnancy; the world premiere was the labor and delivery. After that herstoric event, we were left feeling exhilarated, exhausted, and full of awe, but also a bit at a loss.

Where do we go from here?

We decided to go *within*, and took some time to reflect on what we'd learned. In the fall of 2005, we launched the first ever WGI! Leadership Institute of Arts and Activism for young women, with a dynamic New York–based delegation of artists and activists serving as our inaugural class. These women are now on the road on a WGI! national tour, building a world where young women can, must, and will lead!

Got Issues? Here Are Our Top Ten

There are more than thirty million young women between the ages of eighteen and thirty-five in the United States—Say What?! But our political leadership isn't paying attention. Mainstream media also ignores our concerns (unless you count selling lip gloss, panty shields, or liposuction).

But what would happen if we came together in a creative, compassionate, and organized way? What if there were spaces where we could raise our voices and encourage one another, honor each others' stories, listen to our common (and uncommon) challenges, and wipe each others' tears?

WGI! believes the answer just might help save the planet.

We discovered ten recurring themes in the struggles shared by our sisters across the land. Now, of course, the ten issues we highlight as those we believe are the most pressing for young women in America today in no way cover all of the things that we and our sisters think about, complain about, celebrate about, and *do* something about, but they're a start; we are incubating a ten-point visionary political platform for young women, so be sure to log on to our website (www.wegotissues.org) in 2007 and cast your vote for the issues you believe are most pressing for *you!*

You and This Book

Consider *We Got Issues!* an invitation to celebrate, motivate, rant and rave, be still, kick and scream, laugh and cry. We know that you may not have an hour to read a whole chapter. So read it story by story, bit by bit, on the way to work on the subway, on the toilet with the door locked, in bed, on the plane, on the train. Each chapter has an introduction, our featured bold, courageous, and/or empowered young woman, rants, a set of rituals that you can use to bring each chapter's insights into your own life, and some statistical facts and trends to put it all in context.

Now, let's get one thing clear. You will *not* agree with everything in these pages—none of us who have worked on this labor of love do. So the question is, what will you do with the ones you agree with, and how will you react to the ones you don't? Our request: Be open to learn from all of them. Every single voice in this book has something to offer you, whether it's validation, resonance, and understanding, or anger, fear, and "I told you so."

We hope that these women's experiences can teach you about yourself. We invite you to feel our interconnectedness and be inspired to action.

On behalf of the next wave of women and power, we welcome you into this movement with open arms.

Say who's that next wave woman? I Be! I *Be!* I *BE!!*

Peace,

Rha Goddess and JLove Calderón

Chapter 1

Breath In, Breath Out:
My Life, My Health

I'm not your average girl from your video, and I'm not built like a supermodel, but I learned to love myself unconditionally, because I am a Queen.

—India.Aire

JLove Rants

Since when did our physical and emotional health and well-being come under attack?

From genetically modified foods to pollutants, our bodies are under attack by our environment. Our minds are under attack as well, by negative messages we've gotten from our families, mass media, and, unfortunately, ourselves.

How many women do you know who run themselves ragged (all for a good cause, mind you) until their bodies literally break down? We all know sisters who are sick and need medical attention, but don't have health insurance; they suffer through it, get a little bit better, and then go back to their crazy lifestyle and do it all over again.

Why do we push ourselves so hard, and what will it take to get our temples back in shape? Are we not worthy of a little rest and relaxation?

I'll never forget when my good friend Joanna told me my stressful lifestyle was going to catch up with me one day. I was standing in our kitchen in San Diego, trying to cook an egg in five seconds flat so I could inhale it before running off to work at the homeless shelter.

Ten years later, after being diagnosed with gastritis, a pre-ulcer, and too many gallstones to count, I called Joanna and told her she was right. After doctors removed my gallbladder, I was laying in bed, popping Vicodin for the pain, when a former student visited me and started naming each of the twenty-plus stones they found; some of the names were of nonprofits I worked for, others were collectives I was part of, and a couple were people whose names I'd rather not mention. "I get the point, Rafael," I told him after he hit number seven.

In our fast-paced society, where Starbucks offers a caffeine-boost on every corner, it's no wonder that we young women are in overdrive, racing toward burnout. How much sense does it make rushing to get to yoga classes on time, only to be meditating on your to-do list instead of focusing your heart chakra?

I mean, look at me—it took losing an organ for me to slow down. It wasn't until I was lying on my sickbed, recovering from surgery, I had some time to reflect. I was finally able to hear my internal dialogue, and it sounded like this: "Who am I if I'm not doing something? Am I worthy of happiness when others have nothing?" Yes, ultimately it came down to self-worth. I had spent years putting everything and everyone before myself, and this was the result.

And that's just our bodies, but what about our minds . . . one look at the billboards, magazine covers, and music video's and it is amazing that more of us are not going crazy! Seriously, where do they find these size 0's? And how many of us can afford the luxury of lipo, if you can call it a luxury to pay someone to cut you up and suck you up, all for the sake of fitting into a smaller pair of jeans. That's what's crazy here, that we have bought into this belief that we have to harm our bodies in order to be whole. Tits, ass, lips, toes, and now even designer vaginas! Is anything sacred?

Ladies, it is time to unplug and take an inventory of our physical and emotional state of being. When was the last time you got a massage or had a girls' night? What about just curling up in your favorite sweats with a cup of coffee and some chocolate and reading the book you bought two months ago but just haven't had the time to even look at? If you don't make time in your busy schedule to take care of your body and your mind, in time, your body will force you to pay attention; how many young women do you know who are already grappling with health issues from migraines to stomach problems?

Our health and well-being are paramount to living a good life. What we do to our minds and bodies inside is just as important as what goes on the outside. Are you sleeping well? Are you eating well? Are your relationships healthy?

Take this opportunity to create an ideal vision for your health. Forget about bra and panty size; think about what will give your skin that natural glow, and the spaces and places that fuel you inside.

We have dreams and aspirations to live out, so bite the bullet and schedule that annual physical. Then start to pay attention to how things make you *feel*, and when the answer is not good, do something different.

Oh, yeah, and one other thing—as life starts to pile even more on your plate, practice the art of saying "No!"

Andres Sabogal

Empowered

Jennifer Maya Sabogal

Age:
Alive for 31 years

Cultural Identity:
Scottish-Irish descent

Born:
In Seattle, Washington

Education:
Will be finishing BA this year

Economic Class:
Working/middle class

Marital Status:
Married in September 2005 to the love of my life

Registered to Vote:
Yes

Jennifer Maya Sabogal has worked in the field of health for the past seven years. She has her associate's degree in holistic health care, has studied and implemented permaculture, and has trained and worked as a doula. Jennifer currently works at Planned Parenthood as a reproductive health specialist and abortion counselor and is completing her bachelor's degree at the New College of California. Her thesis, "The Reclamation of Our Reproductive Wisdom," is focused on the political, socioeconomic, religious, and environmental aspects of choice, responsibility, and reproductive sovereignty.

Several years ago, I witnessed a dear friend give birth to her baby boy in the home she had built with her partner. This experience, in contrast to the previous births I had witnessed in the hospital, brought me to my knees in awe. Seeing a woman trust her body to bring a child into the world awoke a deep remembrance. Women are powerful beings! The simple and powerful beauty of the cycle of life brought me to the place of working with women through this transitional time of choice. It was clear to me that this was a path I wanted to follow. When I arrived in the San Francisco Bay Area, I took a doula training course with Natural Resources and soon after started volunteering at Women's Choice Clinic. These two opportunities gave me experiences in being with women through pregnancy and birth as well as supporting women through abortion. I saw these as two sides of the same coin of choice. To become a mother or not is the right of every woman. I believe it is imperative that every child born is a wanted child. Every person born has the right to a healthy environment and community.

❶ What does health look and feel like? What does it mean to be a whole, healthy person?

I believe it has much to do with remembering our connection to the whole. We are interdependent beings. Our health is intimately linked to the health of the Earth, to the health of all beings, to the health of ocean, of soil, of air. Though our society creates the illusion that we are independent, separate creatures, the fact is we are intimately connected to every single cell on this planet. The same life-giving water that passed through the skin of dinosaurs now permeates our flesh and blood. To be whole is to be in balance with our bodies and environment.

❷ What holds us back from being the whole, healthy, vibrant beings we are? What influential presence pressures us to continue this unsustainable rat race?

The structure of our society tries to promote disease on every level of life. The divide-and-conquer mentality that created this country is still a strong force. We now divide from our families, the land, our bodies. We are bombarded with unrealistic demands from our society. From socioeconomic oppression, to corporations and industries spewing their poisons onto Earth and into our bodies, to the limited status quo ideas of what a real woman should look and act like, we are attacked by societal injustices and devastating images every day of our lives. In addition to this assault on our "freedom," we are destroying the Earth in the process. In the U.S., we consume more than a quarter of the world's resources while consisting of 5 percent of the population: a recipe for insanity.

❸ What are some of the common ways in which young women are unhealthy?

Some of the main causes of mental and physical disease in our culture have to do with the lack of community and our disconnection with nature, our family, and our bodies—how to be connected is not taught in our culture. What is taught is how to be a consumer, how to align ourselves with the machine of capitalism, how to be independent instead of interdependent. To heal this separation, we must remember how to cocreate community, how to honor each other, the Earth, and ourselves. Our bodies, like the Earth are to be honored and respected as sacred. Packaged and sold, the pieces of our soul long to unite. The Earth under our feet is alive and breathing. If we are to stand tall in our whole health we must acknowledge and integrate the health of the whole world.

❹ What are some ways we can start to reconnect with the health of this interdependent web of life?

First, slow down. These Western lives are so fast it's hard to feel what is going on. If we want to be actively involved in healing ourselves and the Earth, we must be still enough to listen to what our bodies are telling us, to what the Earth is sharing. When you hear what your body or the Earth is saying, write it down. Start a journal of your journey into health. Meditate, dance, pray, sing, or create art in your unique way. Let the ones in your life know how much you love them; let yourself know how much you love yourself. Plant a garden of food and herbs for nourishment. Check out projects that you can connect or intern with. Use the power of your intentions to create your life from this moment forward.

Words and actions are mantras of manifestation; the more you read and incorporate into your life, the more this reality will be so.

We come into this world as powerful beings and quickly forget our innate wisdom. It is time to remember the beauty and magnificence of being a woman. Honor your blood, honor your cycles; we are the wise ones we have been waiting for.

Please know you are whole and perfect right now. What I mean when I say this is that there is always a place within you that remembers your perfection. Same with the Earth—there are always places on the Earth that are respected and honored in totality. The process is remembering our complete wholeness with this truth.

A New Hand Motion

by Kay Barret

I am looking at the woman next to me &
she thinks I stick both my forefinger
and middle finger down
my
throat.

My mother thought in high school when I fit into a skeletal
size 0 that I tumbled forward into womanhood
with my head in a porcelain toilet bowl,
my chest heaved in the purge of a release.

Inside of my skin there was this toxic waste.
It made all the cute boys shudder and because a cute boy
was <u>essential</u>, I shook up my system
with two fingers
EVERY DAY
after 5 o'clock dinner for two whole years
of my life.

A swell thwarted in the core of my stomach.
In mid-step I felt full.
Full of all the wrong words...
of advertisements that paraded ill ideals of glossed white women

on postered walls...
of everyone's eyes on a lust.
Full of shadowed stories that could only be seen behind the doors of
   bathroom stalls and gagging noises
   while everyone else chattered during lunch.
Full of muscle that built my temple spirit of a body
   that had to
pour out the pounds of fat,
DRILL OUT the pounds of waste
   with just
   a couple of
strokes.

In retrospect, all of my anger had to be
underneath my fingernails.
The very first moment my fingers cruised the adventure
of a woman in her billions of senses, hip bends, and wet
hard glide . . .
I adored filling in the gaps for someone else . . .
not for myself.
To complete someone with my hands
and to cleanse myself with the same basic motion
was a squinted blur:
   a loving person who coincidentally worshipped the "porcelain God."
That was the joke in high school,
everybody laughed.

The punch line was that I confused this with spirituality.

Appetites honed in on music beats, on martial arts sparring.
All were away from my secretly
wrapped safe perversion.
With this,
I hid my own curvature behind an empty frontline.

My jabbing fingers lost their element of control.
They slipped out of the grid of my windpipe after meals

and somehow
somehow i
got hold
of a
pen.

Kay Barret, *ever-shifting sistren/brethren, and fighter and educator and poet, is a twenty-four-year-old, Filipina/Pinay Hapa, queer teaching artist who lives in Chicago. Her words have been thrown out of this world in places like Chicago Cultural Center, Hot House, Batey Urbano, and other spaces of resistance. Salamat to all the pamilya blessing strength each day.*

The health care system wants my identity to become my illness. The system is not set up to help people get well and be successful. If I allowed the system to change me, I would never have my own identity or be successful. The system gave me one path, and the path was sickness. However, I empowered myself to create my own path for success to escape the system.

—Nieta Greene, "The System"

Bodymath

by Elizabeth Brunner

I was strong.

I never had any musical talent to speak of.

My artistic aptitude was overshadowed by my physical tendencies, and my academically inclined mind just didn't shout that loud.

A twenty-foot fall plus bilateral calcaneus (heel) fractures (one open, one not), plus high hopes for recovery, equal traveling for three hours to find a surgeon willing to put them together again.

I was always strong. My body colored my relationship with the physical world. I knew that I could stand on my hands (or let someone else stand on my hands) for a minute or two. My back could double over like a python. My abs contained my reservoir of strength and my calves stood out at right angles when I rose on my toes.

Minus a year as an exchange student in Spain and my physical independence, equals one plate and twelve stainless steel screws.

Soccer, pole vault, Spanish web, trapeze, ring, sports acrobatics, hand balancing, and contortion—my days filled quickly. I was performing about a show a week.

Plus a broken scaphoid and a snapped second metatarsal, makes four broken limbs.

"How old is she, sixteen? Damn kids nowadays, I bet she was on drugs when she jumped off." If I had had a pec left to swing it, or if he had come a little closer, I would have connected my new cast to his fancy doctor's glasses. I had been volunteering for a political nonprofit when the rigging failed.

Minus thirty pounds of muscle, equals two hospitals, three surgeries, three wheelchairs, and many many books.

Without my main handshake, my exterior personality, I felt pity wafting my way. It smelled of defeat. I tried so many ways to swat away the pity, but it came in torrents. I built a new tent, one made of books and curiosity, of life experience and humor. After all, now I could pursue my supermodel career—if only I could ever walk in heels.

Minus my old calves, plus time and a few of those things that age you faster than you thought possible, equal a high school diploma at sixteen.

I ran a little last month. My legs are no longer silken tofu. When my activity level rises again, with it may come arthritis. But, hey—don't look at me like that! Eighteen months later, I'm just as strong, hell, twice as strong as I ever was before.

Elizabeth Brunner *is a seventeen-year-old woman of German-Jewish descent who lives in Portland, Oregon. She is regaining her strength and looking forward to beginning college in fall 2006.*

A Cancer Story

by Anda Maruta Sealey Hoadley Seale

My Aunt Vizma's funeral was on my fourteenth birthday. She died of ovarian cancer. After the funeral, cancer never left my family. Ten years later, my Mom, Brigita, found a pea-sized tumor in her breast. My mom found the tumor one month prior to my wedding but kept it a secret. *I knew something had been bothering her . . .*

Mom had the tumor removed. Cancer disappeared from our family for a couple of years, but returned. Mom told us she had a tumor in her brain and lungs. The doctor gave her one year to live. She lived to meet my first son, Nathaniel, but passed away one month after his first birthday and four months before my second son was born. *I hate cancer. When something good happens in my life, cancer rains on my parade.*

Shortly after my mom's funeral, my mother-in-law told me about genetic testing for breast cancer. I didn't want to hear about cancer. I was doomed. I was going to die of cancer someday, but when? Who knows? Who cares? *Why go ahead and get tested and let cancer rain on my parade again?*

October 2005: I get tested for the BRCA gene mutation. It comes back positive. I have the gene mutation. *I could die of breast or ovarian cancer.* The genetic counselors advise me to let the information sink in. I do. *What am I going to do now?*

The genetic counselors inform me that by the time I am fifty I will have an 85 percent chance of getting breast cancer. They say that I should have my ovaries removed. Ovarian cancer is difficult to detect. By the time they find it, it's too late.

I get my first mammogram in November, the month of my thirty-fifth birthday. Two weeks later a nurse calls me and says they found something suspicious and want me to come back in for another mammogram. *Could I have a tumor? I'm only thirty-five! I'm healthy. I exercise. I eat right.*

At my second mammogram, the radiologists still aren't sure about the tumor, so they test me with an ultrasound. Then they suggest I have an MRI. At this point, I'm thinking, Just remove the breasts! Remove the ovaries! I want to live! *I don't want to be a ticking time bomb.*

The MRI tests come back negative. Huge relief. Two months later I call my doctor and I schedule an oopherectomy to have my ovaries removed.

March 2006: I have my ovaries removed. I am now in menopause at the age of thirty-five. I am taking estrogen and progesterone pills daily so I don't get hot flashes. I plan to have my breasts removed in the summer of 2006.

I'm hoping then cancer will not rain on my parades anymore.

*My name is **Anda Maruta Sealey Hoadley Seale**. My mom and her family immigrated to the U.S. from Latvia at the end of World War II. I was born and raised in Denver, Colorado, where I still live with my husband, Geoff, and sons, Nathaniel and Sandis. I am a second-grade teacher, and have taught in the Denver public school district for more than ten years.*

Each of us has a responsibility to our grandmothers, mothers, sisters, and daughters to educate each other about our health, including our sexual health.
—Katheryn A. Guccione, "Eliminate Cancer!"

Putting Myself First:
Preventing Repeat Messages

by Lea Endres

I can still see four perfect circles on my skin, despite vigorous attempts to wash them off. These circles keep reminding me that two days ago, a paramedic named Dwayne attached my body to a machine in the back of an ambulance in order to monitor my vital signs. The glue he used to attach the plastic patches to my flesh was apparently quite strong, since I can still see round outlines above my right and left breasts, and above the location of each ovary. It feels like my body is visually representing the four directions on a medicine wheel. When I told Dwayne that I'd never been in an ambulance before, he replied, "There's a first time for everything." When I said (through chattering teeth) that I'd never been admitted to a hospital before, he said again, "There's a first time for everything." This made me think about repeat messages.

Though I never have been admitted to a hospital, it actually wasn't my first time in an emergency room. About six years ago, I drove myself to an ER with a pretty severe ankle injury. When a hospital worker saw me hopping on one foot from my car toward the door, he asked if I needed a wheelchair. "No, no, no I'm fine. Really. It's OK." He then offered his arm, which I almost turned down, but finally accepted. As I hopped, pain reverberated through my ankle and up to my teeth. It was absolutely ridiculous. Why didn't I take him up on the wheelchair? Why, two days ago, did I say over and over again to flight attendants, paramedics—anyone who was around—how sorry I was? Over and over, with labored breath, "I'm so sorry, everybody."

The consequences of running and cramming and pleasing and running and running are catching up with me. I need to find value in just resting, just relaxing, just nourishing myself, because I am inherently valuable and worthy of such nourishment.

—Lea Endres, "Putting Myself First: Preventing Repeat Messages"

I'm sorry—a popular phrase on my mental repeat list. Closely associated with "I don't want to bother anyone, that would be an inconvenience; I wouldn't want to trouble anyone, and I shouldn't make a scene." Are you kidding? What the hell was I sorry about two days ago? Sorry for not being fine? Sorry for needing help? Yes, actually, I think I was. I was sorry (really sorry!) for not being fine, because I *should* be fine. It's an inconvenience to others if I'm not fine, so I'll say I'm fine. I should be able to keep going and be productive, so I'm fine. No, really (gasp)—I'm (smile) fine. Fuck fine. I am not fine. Not even close to fine. I am exhausted, depleted, and not, in any way, shape or form, fine. So yes, get me a wheelchair. Or a stretcher.

I have been smiling and being fine for a long, long time. Two days ago I saw that the consequences of this running and cramming and pleasing are catching up with me. Years of prioritizing "productivity" and other people's needs (and my need to be the one to meet other people's needs) over my own health landed me in the hospital after being carried off of a plane on my way back from a meeting. Talk about a wake-up call. The symbology that it was my womb that was freaking out is not lost on me. The center of feminine power screaming at me: Are you there? Are you listening? If I am willing to use and abuse my body in the name of productivity, what else am I willing to use and abuse? I know that how I treat myself is how I treat others, is how I treat the Earth. I know that there is no "out there" that can be fixed, healed, helped, or served if in there is burnt out, stressed out, and sick. I know that it's all connected. I know this. Living each day in light of this knowledge is a different story.

Dwayne wheeled me into the hospital, helped me into a bed in a small room, and left me; about three minutes later I was asked for my insurance card. Um, right. Health insurance? Yet another consequence of my people-pleasing put-myself-last fine-ness—no extra money in my budget for health insurance. So I left. After all that, I left because I had no insurance and couldn't pay the $300 deposit that was required to even sit in that hospital bed. Another wake-up call. Instead of making other people fine or being fine for other people, what if I actually valued my time as my time, and said no to something every once in a while? Imagine that—saying no to others, yes to myself, and being able to afford little things like health care. What a concept.

In the last two days, I've moved quickly into a "reap the benefits from that experience" line of thinking. Again, devaluing just resting, just relaxing, just nourishing myself, because I *am* inherently valuable and worthy of such nourishment. But the circles on my skin seem to be mocking this activity—reminding me that all my motion is secondary to the simple truth that my life is fragile, and my health dictates how much I will do today. And how much I will do tomorrow. I know that when my current markings fade, it will be challenging to keep the same level of focus on my health or on putting myself first. And I also know that, on the scales of severity, I have had a fairly gentle warning. May I listen well and need no repeat messages.

Lea Endres is a human rights educator and artist finally reclaiming her own right to personal and economic health. She is currently living in Los Angeles.

Yoga Warriors Fight Depression

by Julia Neuber

When I found out about yoga, I was at a holistic spa in Brazil with my mother. I was nineteen and overcoming depression followed by panic syndromes: hard times indeed. Luckily, the spa was very uplifting with a kind staff and activities such as gardening and meditation. The first thing that I noticed immediately after my first yoga class was the feeling of utter relaxation. When I came back from my short vacation, I was surprised to find out that the gym I was attending was offering yoga classes. Unlike at the spa, the classes at the gym were far more challenging and vigorous; I hated them! But my ambition got the best of me and I decided to give it another try. This time, I practiced before I got to class. Afterwards, I realized that it was going to take more than a couple of classes to adapt. I also realized that even trying to overcome those obstacles made me feel more confident. I was not depressed anymore; instead, I was full of hope and plans for the future.

My teacher, Andre De Rose, was very important in my evolution both as a practitioner and a person. When I was ready, I wanted to share the benefits of yoga with others the way Andre did with me. I started giving private yoga classes. Everything was great until my mother died. I was devastated, and got depressed again. The only thing that I was doing was practicing yoga. My depression lasted for six months. It was hard to get out of bed, but when I was thinking about myself doing poses, learning something from my students, I *wanted* to get up.

Through that journey I found out that everything changes—even the hardest things. I learned to accept and acknowledge change. Yoga helps because when you practice, you feel a connection with your body, mind, and breath. You face your body *as it is*, and you start to watch the changes in your mind. Yoga postures stimulate your body's chakras and makes your mind more flexible. When something doesn't work the way we want, we don't stop to judge anyone or think how miserable we are; we take action instead.

I am now blessed with teaching yoga seven times a week. I share yoga poses and everything I have learned: self-actualization and detachment. I want my students to sweat, work hard, accept their bodies, and overcome their obstacles.

We can take care of ourselves by eating healthy, and practicing yoga with a positive attitude. We can convert negative thoughts into pure energy. We can become the definition of the word "warrior."

Julia Neuber discovered yoga in São Paulo, Brazil, six years ago; she is currently teaching in New York. She is a Sivananda and Om Yoga Center certified yoga instructor. Her goal is to teach people how to be in the present moment and achieve self-discovery.

It is quite an adventure, this "human" experience. The life journey here on Earth is a journey of remembrance—of realizing our innate infinite potential. My experience has been joyful, painful, loving, irritating. I've been crazy with passion or anxiety. In my early twenties (human years), I discovered that realizing my consciousness was a full-time job. Consciously creating my experience was the only thing that made sense. Otherwise I would only be a victim of my external circumstances—and I was creating those external circumstances, too, without awareness.

—Lalania Simone Carrillo, "Goddess Training 101"

That's What Friends Are For

by Deanna Kubota

Desperation filled her eyes with tears. "Give us the knife." "Noooo!" A reluctant sob. I grasped her flailing arms through the protective sheath of a blue Nike jacket.

The ambulance took her away. Teachers told us, "Go back to class."

We sneered and said, "Fuck off."

You didn't prevent this. That was our friend you just took away, not just some delinquent. She has a name. "It's OK." No! It's not. She carved some letters in her skin because she couldn't reach out. "Fuck you!" we scream. Fuck your pills and counseling! Choke on the forms we kids need to fill out with an "adult by your side."

Deanna Kubota, eighteen, is an angst-riddled Japanese/Yugoslavian teen who lives in Maui.

We are to live in our hearts,
not in our heads
Together we must cry and laugh
—Gandana Sharma, "Fire Blown"

Ritual of Empowerment

Actively supporting our physical heath and well-being means making concrete changes in our daily lives.

Commit to Your Physical Health

Create an affirmation for your physical health and hang it up somewhere you can see it. Make sure you do the following activities every day (even if it means you have to write them on your calendar or program them into your PDA):

- Drink water (at least three to four eight-ounce glasses a day).
- Exercise daily (even a brisk twenty-minute walk).
- Laugh. E-mail yourself funny jokes that you can open while you're at work; become the office Director of Mirth, and every morning hand out comics, pictures, stories, or jokes.
- Step outside and get some fresh air for at least fifteen minutes.

Start wherever you can, and then build in the other practices one day at a time.

The Art and Healing of Storytelling: Creating Your Red Tent

There is a long and sacred legacy of women healing themselves and each other through storytelling. Back in the day, women created sacred time and space where they could share their herstories in laughter, song, tears, prayer, and silence. Together, let's reclaim this ritual for the health and vitality of ourselves, our families, and our communities.

Inspired by Anita Diamant's award-winning book, we invite you and your closest friends to a create a Red Tent. Ask each woman to bring red fabric or pillows and a personal artifact—something that is important to them (a piece of clothing, a rock from a meaningful spot, something that someone special gave them, a photo, etc.).

Find a comfortable space and decorate it with materials that make you happy. Try to have red fabrics cascade down from the ceiling to create a tentlike feel. Arrange a circle of pillow seats for your guests. In the middle, create a space for fresh flowers, candles, and the personal artifacts.

When your guests arrive, greet them and invite them into your sacred space. Once everyone is inside the tent, ask them to put their artifacts in the center near the flowers and candles. If they have brought fabric and pillows, have them add them to tent as needed.

Invite each guest to share a story (don't forget to include yourself). They can speak about what they brought in and why it is significant to them, or share something else. The only rule here is to share with your heart.

See what unfolds.

We Got Stats!

➡️ Women are generally considered to hold a more negative body image than men. As a result, **body dissatisfaction among women has been labeled a "normative discontent."**
—Tanya Davison and Marita McCabe. *Sex Roles: A Journal of Research* (2005)

➡️ In 2003, 79% of women age 18 and over reported a Pap smear within the past 3 years. Among women between 25 and 44, **Pap smear use was lowest for women with less than a high school education** (72%) and highest for women with at least some college education (91%).
—Centers for Disease Control and Prevention National Center for Health Statistics (2004); National Committee on Vital and Health Statistics (2005); U.S. Department of Health and Human Services (2006)

➡️ Each year, eating disorders such as **anorexia nervosa and bulimia nervosa** affect millions of Americans, 85% to 90% of whom are teens and young adult women. —National Mental Health Association (1999)

➡️ Approximately **12 million women in the United States experience depression every year**—roughly twice the rate of men.
National Mental Health Association. "MHIC: Mental Illness and the Family: Mental Health Statistics" http://www.nmha.org/infoctr/factsheets/15.cfm

➡️ Women report attempting suicide about **3 times as often as men.**
—World Health Organization (2002)

➡ Approximately **80% of women want to lose weight.** —National Organization for Women Foundation

➡ **Average women vs. Barbie:**

Stats	Average woman	Barbie
Height	5'4"	6'0"
Weight	145 lbs.	101 lbs.
Dress size	11 to14	4
Bust	36" to 37"	39"
Waist	29" to 31"	19"
Hips	40" to 42"	33"

—Anorexia Nervosa and Related Eating Disorders, Inc.

➡ During one act of intercourse, a woman's risk of contract-ing **gonorrhea** may be as high as 90%, while the risk to a man is between 20% and 30%. The **risk of contracting HIV has been estimated to be 8 times higher** from man to woman as it is from woman to man.
—The Kaiser Family Foundation (1998)

➡ The percentage of females without insurance (14.4 %) is slightly lower than the percentage of males (16.8 %). However, **women of color are more likely than white women to lack coverage:** 10.4% of non-Hispanic white females were uninsured, compared to 17.8% of African-American females, 18.5% of Asian-American females, and 29.6% of Hispanic females. —U.S. Department of Health and Human Services (2005)

Chapter 2

From (A)theist to (Z)en
The Spirit I'm In

Rha Rants

Close your eyes and take a deep breath. Whether you're sitting on the train, riding in a car, or reading this at your desk, just take a moment to breathe and reconnect with your life force.

Let your breath flow, and simply become aware of the soles of your feet firmly planted, of the expansion and contraction of your lungs, and of the subtle beating of your heart.

Some of us call it Allah, Jehovah, Yemaya, Jesus, God, Goddess, Spirit, Creator, the Universe, or Nothing. The *I AM* is called many things, but its true essence remains constant. And this wonderful, loving force can be tapped in so many ways. In its purest form, this force brings peace, clarity, joy, abundance, and light. Its greatest desire is to give, nurture, and create. Yes, all roads do inevitably lead here.

To tell the truth, I am not a fan of organized religion. As I watch the world around me, the disease, poverty, senseless greed, and violence—all set to the soundtrack of "God Bless America" or "Put God first" or "First of all, I want to thank God for this Grammy"—my immediate response is, "Give me a break."

I love God: mother god, father god, the divine spirit, the creator—I know this force and I have felt its hand in my life. But what thirty years of pulpit and pillow chasing has shown me is that my relationship with God is about the direct connection I have with this force, through my own heart and voice, and how I choose to *live* as a result of that connection. It's not about my reliance on someone else to dictate who or what it is for me.

Any religion that sees its followers as superior or uses faith to subjugate another raises fundamental questions about God's presence for me.

As we experience these latest crises in humanity—from the war in Iraq to Hurricane Katrina to mass rape and murder in Darfur—more blood has been spilled in the name of God than perhaps at any other time in history. As governments and individuals do battle over beliefs and values, love gently whispers, "There are many truths, many perspectives, many points of view."

I believe spirituality is the practice of being inspired, and when we are inspired, we are in love: with ourselves, with life, and with our dreams. Love, when experienced in its truest form, is infinite. And faith that is rooted in love has nothing to prove, protect, or defend. Love is the food of our soul. And our soul lives to be inspired.

As we explore the idea of faith, the larger question that we must begin to ask ourselves is, What are we believing *in?* Because what we believe is what we manifest.

I believe in love.
I believe in the wisdom of nature.
I believe in purpose.

There are the things we know we believe, and then there is another world, an interior, sometimes hidden world that holds a whole host of beliefs that we may not even be aware of. Some of these beliefs generate love and some generate fear.

When we slow down, listen to our breath, and feel our truth, we gain a wealth of wisdom and insight. We all have access to this wisdom through prayer, meditation, divine scripture, chanting, yoga, inspirational movement, or just good ol'-fashioned silence.

I believe in the interconnectedness of humanity.
I believe in silence, in stillness, and in breath.
I believe in the inherent goodness of all people.

I feel my greatest spiritual practice is to keep my heart open. To allow my heart, which holds my deepest truth, to lead the way. To trust my heart as my primary line of communication. To quiet all the other noise and move closer to the God in me.

Inevitably, when I can do that, great things happen: I grow; I am able to go to a deeper, more authentic place in my relationships; I am able to find peace and feel the spirit moving in my life.

When we stand for our highest truth, a sense of order naturally and organically comes into our lives. Things that do not serve us miraculously begin to fall away. Sometimes the losses are painful, sometimes they're easy, but ultimately they are liberating. And the things that elevate and encourage us are drawn even closer.

When we stand for our highest truth we are also tested, because the creative forces want to make absolutely sure that we are ready to receive their responsibilities and riches.

I believe in second, third, and sometimes even fourth chances.
I believe in seasons, reasons, tests, lessons, and lifetimes.
I believe in surrendering and letting go—when I can muster the courage to do it.

How do you embrace your spirit?

Many of us have been through our share of trauma, and we know that some of the wounds still have not healed. Though we have managed to survive, some of us have left pieces of ourselves behind.

How do we begin to confront those scars—gently?

With tender love and care?

How do we remember our spirits?

This chapter is dedicated to your soul, and the divine inheritance of grace that allows us to face any challenge and move right on through to the other side— triumphant.

Courageous

Immaculée Ilibagiza

Immaculée Ilibagiza was born in Rwanda and studied engineering at the National University. She lost most of her family during the 1994 genocide. Four years later, she immigrated to the United States and began working for the United Nations in New York. She established the Left to Tell Foundation to help others heal from the long-term effects of genocide and war. She is the best-selling author of Left to Tell: Discovering God Amidst the Rwandan Holocaust, *(Hay House) and the subject of the documentary film* Diary of Immaculée. *Immaculée lives on Long Island with her husband, Bryan Black, and their children, Nikeisha and Bryan Jr.*

Age:
36
Cultural Identity:
From Rwanda
Born:
In Rwanda, Africa
Education:
University level
Occupation:
Author and public speaker
Economic Class:
Average
Marital Status:
Married
Registered to Vote:
Not yet

❶ When was the first time you remember believing in something?

From the time I was a person who could think, I was praying. I thought about God and I knew He was there.

❷ How did your upbringing influence your spirituality?

My parents prayed every night as a family, kneeling down together in front of the cross. I know that we had to keep quiet during a prayer. That was the moment I respected most in my life; I don't remember when they told me to respect it, but I knew I had to. My parents spoke about God and being good for God all the time; I knew I had to do the same.

I grew up questioning my parents on the origin of everything, and the origin of God; I remember it troubled me for a while to imagine God being eternal. I never got an answer, and later when I heard about apparitions of the Virgin Mary in the world, I got to understand and to see the existence of miracles. I was relieved because I wanted to make sense of everything in the human imagination, but with God I got to know that everything was mysterious and possible.

❸ Describe the moment when your faith became yours.

My faith became mine when I learned about the apparitions of Mary—at a certain level. Finally, my faith became real during my hiding in the bathroom for three months from the genocide in Rwanda. I knew then for sure, I could never be an atheist, for I have felt God to another level.

When I was forced to be silent for those months, I had nothing else to hold onto except God. As they were searching to kill me, I begged God to help and do a miracle, and He did for sure, many times. Sometimes I was faced by thoughts of doubt about the existence of God, but the signs were too many to convince me.

I remember telling God, "God, I never needed you in my life as I do now. If you are there, please open the door because I am knocking and you said you would open if anyone knocks." And He answered me always.

He spoke to me in dreams about real things that were going to happen; He offered me the grace to forgive those who were killing me, and I cherish that.

So here the relationship with God was clear and clean; I didn't need any religion to love God. I spent with Him three months conversing, transforming, and it was enough to know that He is the Faithful Friend, the one sees every corner of my heart, who helps me to do everything in my life today—I mean every second of the day when no one else knows where I am or what I am doing or going through. I see Him in everyone and everything He created, and that is enough for me.

❹ What is the most difficult thing you have had to overcome, and how did your faith help you?

The hardest thing was to loose my parents and my two brothers during the genocide in Rwanda. Not only them: losing my neighbors, my schoolmates, my friends, losing every belonging I had, the house, the pictures, the clothes and books and every note I loved. It was a horrible time and yet I felt whole inside because I understand that God is all I needed to survive all this, that He loved me, that my friends and my parents are not lost, they are just in heaven. I took a long time trying to understand what that love meant, love that is bigger that mountains and valleys as described in the Bible, love that is sweeter and more real than that of our own parents. I spent hours in meditations, contemplating those realities.

I tried to understand and to take seriously Heaven: If they say that Heaven is more beautiful than earth, if they say that the roads in heaven are made of diamonds and gold, that there is no pain in heaven, I tried to visualize that, and I wanted to accept it as real. I was able to accept the death of my loved ones because I knew they are not in a bad place, and I can't be selfish to want them where I want them to be, here with me. You know, it didn't stop tears, the same way we send our children to school knowing it is good for them, but yet we cry because we will miss them. I had and I still have hysterical moments of tears for missing my loved ones but at the end I tell God, "Let your will be done, you know better," and I feel OK despite the tears.

❺ Do you see a difference between faith, spirituality, and religion?

I don't see any difference. The true love has the same flavor even to those who genuinely don't know God but who have holy love in their hearts.

❻ What would you say to other young women who want to incorporate faith and spirituality into their lives?

I would tell them, Go for it, the common language is love, if you go there with love, with the ambition to love better, you will learn a lot. You don't have to take everything everyone is telling you; your heart will tell you what is needed in your life, you don't have to be judgmental. But no matter what, when it comes to faith and spirituality we learn a lot and the common goal is to feel one with God.

❼ What would you say to young women who feel very challenged by their current spiritual path?

I would tell them to listen to their inner voice better; your heart is your path. Just remember one thing: Let love be a measurement of how you make your decisions in life, and you can never go wrong. Take time to listen to God inside, let Him be your number-one relationship. If you are seeking genuinely you will find Him; just be honest, sincere in whatever you don't understand, even in weakness. Open up and tell God what your fears are and dare to ask him for help. I bet the answer will always come.

❽ What does a spiritually empowered young woman look like?

A spiritually empowered woman looks happy always; her joy comes from within, she is not attached to anything living, but her number-one love is God and He can never disappoint or reject—the base of your life is that solid and unshakable. The spiritually empowered woman wants the best for others, and she gets her blessings by wishing good to others and helping them. She is not jealous or angry; she is forgiving, because she understand how essential it is to feel good inside and how to please God. She knows she is here for a purpose and she is proud of herself.

❾ How do we as a human family overcome the perceived challenges associated with having different faiths?

By practicing love as we understand it from the inside, not as it is written somewhere outside. By loving as we love ourselves, as God loves us, and practicing

His pure commandments. Humans have become this kind of smart, blind family that is looking for what they have already, but they are too smart and proud, they can't accept the fact that they have it so easy. And in searching what we have already, what we know already, our ego and our pride don't get that satisfaction until we hurt others, until we find the wrong ones. And what we have always and are still searching for is love, and how to put God first.

Smokin' an L with Jesus

by Adrienne Maree Brown

i have realized, at the ripe old age of twenty-seven, that there are a couple of versions of heaven:

1. there is the heaven for people who love harps and choir music. they bop on elevators and often wish their hair was more flowy. i can't get around to aiming for this one, and it keeps me from bowing my head often enough, i'm sure.

2. there is a heaven that involves one long, perfect, magic-hands massage. i dare say i pray for this one daily.

3. there is a heaven in which we humans finally evolve to a place of inner and outer peace, and treat each other with respect, live in trust and freedom, and want for nothing but good work. i act like i live there and hold no small measure of pride in my surprise at proof to the contrary.

4. there is a heaven that is a beach in the marshall islands where i healed once—where the sand comes out against the ocean and in every direction, as far as the eye can see, you can look. you can watch the rains come hours away, and you can watch the far side of the sunset, and you can see the very first glimpse of the earth turning toward that same sun but we call it new and it constantly amazes, and the wind is

warm and the sharks are near and when night comes, she brings a million stars to tell you her stories.

5. and then there is the one i have found on earth: a friday night, a late-night date with myself, watching science fiction shows, eating oreos, with a sip of whiskey and a bit of puff and no clothes anywhere near me and no work and no phone ringing and absolutely nothing, in this room that i don't want here.

6. and then there is my ultimate heaven, the one in which i get to spend a lot of time on the beach, in peace, often sitting alone to think, but sometimes getting to choose someone to sit back and smoke an l with, and ask my big questions to. my short list includes every major martyr or religious figure, writer of perfect songs, prophet, revolutionary, and lover i've ever known or known of. i would like to start with jesus, given the great obsession and oppression of my time, based on poor interpretations of his short life. and then nina simone, to ask how she was able to keep singing when some days break you of sound. and i would probably want to sing a song with her, because i've lost all shame and besides, it's my heaven. and then a panel of inventors, to ask what it feels like to have a completely new idea in a world that runs from change. and then i would love to sit down with the creation force, in whatever form i can handle, just to say why fifty times, for closure. and that is my list of heavens.

Adrienne Maree Brown is the executive director of the Ruckus Society (www.ruckus.org). She cut her national organizing teeth as cofounder of the League of Young Voters, where she created training and communications programs and coedited How to Get Stupid White Men Out of Office. *Her work focuses on power and pleasure. She is also a writer, singer-songwriter, traveler, and organizational developer.*

Ramadan Love Letter

by Rhian Kohashi O'Rourke

I fell in love with you right after I accidentally popped a date in my mouth.

I was fasting, in solidarity with my Muslim friends (and secretly because I was more Muslim than anything else, but was afraid to convert). Najla, my Egyptian friend, called and asked what I was doing for *iftar*. My tummy grumbled, mouth arid, body shriveled up like a prune.

"Come. We are almost done preparing *iftar*," she said.

You were cooking. Only the back of your shaved head greeted me, as you busily prepared *muglobeh*. But you heard the door close, turned and warmly welcomed me, *"Ramadan Kareem."*

I stared at your dark eyebrows, more dramatic than any I had ever seen before. No matter how many times I had seen you in the past three years, they still threw me off. They danced on your face. Made you look so severe when you were concentrating. Jumped to the top of your forehead when you were excited. Traveled all over when you were drinking (but not this month; it was Ramadan)—especially as you passed out rounds to your friends, saying "cheers" like a gregarious motherfucker (I mean mofo; during the holy month we weren't sup- posed to swear or even think bad thoughts).

I sliced veggies into baby cubes. The tomatoes burst with seeds and fluid. Everything got more frenzied as we neared *maghreb*. Four min-

{ 41 }

utes seventy-five seconds. You frantically placed special dates from Saudi Arabia on the table. As soon as you released them, I picked one up and popped it in my mouth and chewed away at its blissfully sweet, mushy insides. "This is what heaven is." I swallowed most of it before I realized what I had just done.

"Oh my god! Fuck!" I exclaimed (and then "shit" in my mind because I had just sworn out loud). They turned to my panicked face.

"I ate a date! *Wallahai*, I didn't mean to. I can't believe it. What's wrong with me? I fasted the whole day to waste it like this?"

They all just stared.

But you, you put your hand on my back, right between my shoulders. "*Habibty*, it's a gift from god. Allah just blessed you with this date. You were meant to have it."

And that's when I knew that Allah had blessed me with much more than that date—Allah blessed me with you.

Iftar refers to the evening fast-breaking meal during the Islamic month of Ramadan
Muglobeh is a popular rice-based spicy Arabic dish with cauliflower and either meat or chicken
Ramadan Kareem is a greeting used during the holy month of Ramadan
Maghreb is the evening call to prayer
Wallahai means "I swear to God" in Arabic
Habibty is a term of affection meaning "my love" in Arabic
Allah translated from Arabic to mean God

Rhian Kohashi O'Rourke *is a twenty-four-year-old Japanese- and Irish-American activist writer who was born in Zimbabwe and spent most of her childhood in India and Egypt. Rhian freelanced for the* Jordan Times *and* JO magazine *while she was living in Amman, and currently works on poverty issues at a progressive think tank in Washington, D.C. She lives in Virginia.*

What Does Jesus Look Like?

by Rosa Alicia Clemente

I was raised in the Catholic Church. From the moment I was placed under this religious institution, I was put in a situation where my savior would never look like me. For me, Jesus Christ was a white man with blond hair and blue eyes. Much of my high school years were spent going to church and confessing my teenage sins to a white man who would absolve me of those sins and tell me to pray to a white woman, Virgin Mary, who in turn would save my soul. By the time I was fourteen I thought all white men and women did was save people; the only man of color I saw in an position of authority was my dad, and *papi* did not look like Jesus.

While for many, our spiritual path gives us strength, the Catholic Church robbed me of mine; it made me question why Jesus, God, and the Holy Spirit did not look like me. One day after school, I went to my best friend's house and noticed a picture of Jesus Christ on the wall; unlike in my house, Jesus in this picture was black. I stared at the picture and that image seared into my consciousness. That Sunday when I went to church, I was so conflicted; it didn't make sense! When you are brainwashed by a religious institution and contradictions arise that conflict with your spirituality, it's hard to see the truth.

That Sunday would be my last as a Catholic. Although this decision caused some family schisms, I realize now that it was one of the best personal decisions I could have ever made to save my spirit, my soul, the essence of who I am.

As a search for spiritual lessons for my daughter, I have committed myself to focus on the readings of different religions. While reading the teachings of Jesus Christ, I have learned what I believe is the truth of this person. I understand the fullness of him as a man in a specific historical time: an African revolutionary who walked with the dispossessed.

So when a spokesperson for the Catholic League condemned Kanye West for portraying Jesus Christ on the cover of *Rolling Stone*, and proceeded to call him and the magazine "moronic," I ask: Was it wrong for Moses to be portrayed by Charlton Heston, a gun-touting member of the National Rifle Association? What about the hoopla surrounding the Mel Gibson movie *The Passion of the Christ?* I do not recall similar outrage from the Catholic League when the actor Jim Caviezel was on every cover of every major magazine. What about the many thousands of white men who have portrayed Jesus Christ in the last hundred years of cinema and television?

But I am not naïve. It is not about seeing Jesus in a contemporary light. Renderings of what people believe to be Jesus Christ have been around forever. The problem for the Catholic League and many white Christians, who will start coming out of the woodwork to condemn Kanye, is that Kanye West as a black man does not represent their revisionist history of who Jesus was.

So once again, brother Kanye West has used the mainstream media to shake up white America: score two for Hip-Hop culture. It may seem small and insignificant to many folks, but as someone who believed for years that white men were my spiritual saviors, seeing that cover of *Rolling Stone* was a reaffirmation of my teenage decision.

Late last night, as I was walking in my 'hood, Flatbush, I was singing in my head, "To the hustlers, killers, murderers, drug dealers, even the strippers (Jesus walks with them), to the victims of welfare feel we living in hell here, hell yeah (Jesus walks with them), God show me the way because the Devil try to break me down (Jesus Walks with me)." When I walked into my house and picked up my baby girl, Alicia, I showed her the picture of Kanye on the cover of *Rolling Stone.* She looked and smiled. I laid her down in her crib and she stared at the picture of Kanye that I put above her. She fell asleep knowing that not only does Jesus walk with her, but Jesus looks like her, too.

Rosa Alicia Clemente *is a Bronx-born black Boricua. From her two parents, she learned to be happy, angry, innovative, important, and loving. She is motivated by her daughter, Alicia-Maria, to make a better world starting in her 'hood of Flatbush, Brooklyn, and her life is better with her man, Justice, who always makes her laugh.*

The middle of 2005 found me in the middle of
an unease so heavy, they call it depressing.
I'd prayed my way out of it, clad in white,
beads on my neck and around my belly.
I knew love was what I needed.
To give and get it.
To walk through fear with it.
To manifest it.
—Suheir Hammad, "Thursday, January 5th"

Your eyes shine amber sundrops looking thru from
ancient worlds
Your spirit a Jaguar
Your heart a Renegade warrior
Your smile a pearl . . .
Your tears heal the pain of the children
—Audrey Pullen, "To the Women of Zapoteca"

Satan Whispers in My Ear

by K. Strickland

They told me when I was little, "This is the way, this is the light." They told me that while they grabbed me and held me down. I have seen the way and the light now through the Disciples' dick.

You want to talk about Jezebel and Mary. You who give a woman two options, virgin or whore, and then you make the decision for her.

I was raised in the Southern Baptist tradition, learned the Bible, taught the ways. I learned the importance of appearance. I learned that a woman that who dressed a "certain" way was a "certain" way. I am taught that Eve was a good little girl, played with God's creatures in fields of flowers until one day, her treacherous heart coveted something, and she took it. When I was a kid, I imagined that after she succumbed to the devil's evil ways, she pranced around nude, touching herself and spreading ashes around her eyes. She would sway up to Adam and lure him with her naughty eyes. That's the only way Adam was tempted, right? He could have withstood, but Eve looked too damn good eating that juicy apple, right?

Age 13: A girl without makeup or artifice, who follows and believes in the way and the light, can tempt and be held accountable for her own rape.

Age 14: A girl with heathen eyes says "fuck you" to the church— you made me this way. "Do not lust after her beauty in your heart, nor let her allure you with her eyelids." —Proverbs 6:25

Age 18: There is a distinction growing up here. There is the holy and the unholy. They try to place her into a mold, castigate her, and hold her as an example while throwing the stones.

Age 22: There is sanctity in the Tao that reaches into my soul and sets pain and hurt aside; it teaches me what the Bible tried to. "In dwelling, live close to the ground. In thinking, keep to the simple. In conflict, be fair and generous. In governing, don't try to control. In work, do what you enjoy. In family life, be completely present." "Knowing others is intelligence; knowing yourself is true wisdom. Mastering others is strength; mastering yourself is true power."

Age 25: They tell me that Satan is whispering in my ear. My question is, When did he become so wise?

K. Strickland is a twenty-six-year-old multicultural Americanized mutt. She is a lover of all things artistic who hails from the Sautee Nacoochee area in northern Georgia. She has recently started writing again, and hopes to have more work out soon—if she doesn't delete it first.

When Israeli soldiers refuse to follow insane, unjust orders, that's truth. When a woman who loves another woman pledges their love in public, defies the law, and weds, that's truth. When a dam comes down and frees a river, when a bird is saved, when someone learns to read, when the sick get healed, when we learn compassion, when we learn to forgive, when we know we are one race, the human race . . . That's truth.
—Kathryn Blume, "Truth"

She Called Me Home

by Julia Ahumada Grob

On the crest of a Bolivian mountain, on a lake that lives in the clouds, I met God. I pressed my hand to her footprint and felt her presence. The sun beating against my back, kissing me, blessing me, reminding me: She was calling me home.

Incan folklore explains that Pachamama, the earth Goddess, was born on Isla del Sol, a tiny island in the middle of Lake Titicaca. If you go there, you will find her first footprint on land. Raised a liberal Jew, I had attended Hebrew school for years, had a bat mitzvah and confirmation—but never before had I felt God's presence. In that moment I understood that she was something beyond. Intangible, she lived in the beauty of the natural earth, which surrounds me.

Mafer Efun Elegua—the drums salute Elegua, the orisha who opens up opportunity. We leave candy at crossroads, spit rum in his face, blow cigar smoke in his mouth. I'm dancing and singing with the chorus, hypnotized by this new spirituality. Lost in the sound and movement, my head begins to get hot; my eyes become big enough to take everything in. Suddenly I'm taken back to Lake Titicaca—I feel Pachamama surround me again. I find heaven in a San Jose backyard.

I am woman,
Muslimah.
I am that voice that cries
injustice through your
dreams at night.
I represent the feminine
side of God.

—Adeeba Rama,
"What Are You?"

{ 48 }

"Does this mean you aren't Jewish anymore?" my mom asks me when I tell her I will be initiated into Santeria. I have to explain that Judaism, to me, is a cultural background, an ethnicity. Like my other half—the Chilean one—my mother's Jewish roots define me culturally and ethnically. They have never defined me religiously. Judaism often speaks a language that does not move me. Beyond Israeli songs and dances that I loved in Hebrew school, I find no universal truths in the Judaism I have been taught. It doesn't account for the fantastical nature of the world I am experiencing; for the dreams that teach me about the people in my life, shocking me when weeks later they come true; for the moments of magic, of faith, that I experience daily. In Santeria, I find space to communicate with my ancestors, who I learn are fully present with me at all times. I finally feel my gramps's wisdom surround me. I feel him at my college graduation, blessing me as I walk through the historic gates. When my dear friend Luis passes, he stays with me in my room, hugs and kisses me, and reminds me to believe in love. In, return I leave him a glass of water, sweet rum, and incense to guide his path. I soon learn that when I'm in need I can always run to the river or ocean to cry my tears to Ochun or Yemaya, and they will bring clarity.

I sometimes wonder how she found me. What did this spirit know of a mixed Jewish-Chilean Hip-Hop head from New York City? How did she know I would find peace in African religion?

Despite our ancestry, we never know where our spirits are truly from. We find our calling in strange and unusual sources. As for me, I found mine in a kiss shared between the sun, the land, and the water, on the island that birthed the Goddess.

Julia Ahumada Grob is a twenty-three-year-old, Chilean and Jewish performer, writer, educator, and activist from New York City. She can often be found dancing to the rhythm of ancient drums while learning to trust in love.

Ritual of Empowerment

What do you believe in? What are the things that truly inspire you? And what are the things that scare you to death? Let's take an inventory.

The Spiritual Garden

At the top of the first sheet, write "Inspiring Beliefs." Set the timer for five minutes. Write down everything you believe in, that inspires you, brings you joy, makes you laugh, and gives you peace. Don't censor yourself. Go as fast as you can and find as many beliefs as you can that *really* feed your soul. When time is up, take a moment in silence to look over your list. Take each item in fully; allow yourself to feel the connection you have to these beliefs. Notice the ones that give you the most energy—put a star next to them.

Now reset the timer for another five minutes and move to your second sheet of paper. Write the heading: "Limiting Beliefs." In the same uncensored way, write down every belief you can think of that creates fear, sadness, anger, pain. Go as fast as you can and find as many beliefs as you can that *really* challenge you.

When time is up, take a moment and review your list. Take each item in fully; allow yourself to feel the disconnection you have to these beliefs. Notice the ones that give you the most negative energy—put a star next to them.

Now bring both lists together; we are going to first weed, and then seed, our garden. For this part of the ritual you will need a book of matches; a large ashtray or bowl; and a small glass of water. (If you have access to a fire pit, that's even better.) You will also want a large sheet of paper, markers, and crayons.

Go to your Limiting Beliefs list and count how many items you have starred; take another clean sheet of paper and tear it into the same number of pieces. Then, on each piece, write one limiting belief. Now set up your bowl or ashtray and, one by one, light each piece of paper on fire. As the pieces burn, feel yourself letting go and releasing all the limitation these beliefs have had in your life. If you are doing this with a partner or a group, make sure everyone has a chance to do this before you move on. If you want to, say "I release" and then state the limiting belief as each piece burns. Once the burning is done, give yourself a moment of silence.

Now, move on to your Inspiring Beliefs. Using the large piece of paper with the markers and crayons, create an artistic representation of your starred beliefs. Find a room or corner within your living space and hang this display. If you already have a designated area for your faith and spiritual practices, you can hang it there. If not, let this display help you create one. Over the next week, see if you can find something in nature that represents each of the starred beliefs on your list. Collect them and bring them back to your spiritual corner. As part of your daily rituals, spend at least five minutes a day in this area connecting with your inspirational beliefs. Take this opportunity to feed your soul and your spirit.

We Got Stats!

➡ The ratio of females to males who identify with **different faith groups** varies over a wide ratio. Only 38% or 39% of Seventh-Day Adventists, Buddhists, and Muslims are women; 55% or more of the persons identifying with the Episcopalian, Methodist, Pentecostal, or Presbyterian denominations are female.
—Bruce A. Robinson. "Religious Identification in the U.S." (2001)

➡ The Unitarian Universalist religion is the first major faith group with a **majority of female clergy**. Women have had equal and sometimes superior roles within Wiccan and Neopagan groups. —Bruce A. Robinson. "Religious Identification in the U.S." (2001)

➡ Women are about **twice as likely as men to be fully spiritually committed**, both in the general population (17% of women and 8% of men) and within faith communities (22% and 11%). —D. Winseman and Albert L. Min, Gallup Poll (2003)

➡ According to a U.S. Census report from February 2004, 56,000 women are working as clergy in the U.S. Yet **churches are fraught with all the equity issues** found in the greater society they serve. —Kelly Westhoff, Minnesota Women's Press (2004)

➡ According to the most recent statistics compiled by the Association of Theological Schools of the United States and Canada, the **number of women entering seminary school has risen** every year since 1999. In 2003, 20,199 women were enrolled in divinity schools across the U.S.; women made up 33% of the seminary student body. —Kelly Westhoff, Minnesota Women's Press (2004)

➧ Religious participation is one of the strongest factors associated with **increased civic and political involvement.** —Amy Caiazza, Institute for Women's Policy Research

➡ The total number of faith groups in the U.S. cannot be calculated. The value depends upon exactly how one defines "faith group" or "religion." **Perhaps we can say that every person's religion is, to somewhat, degree unique.** Thus there are over 200 million religions in the U.S.

—Bruce A. Robinson. Religioustolerance.org

Chapter 3

Operation Outrage
The Big ISMS

Some days when I walk into the office and people ask me how I'm doing I want to say, "Pretty fuckin' colonized!"
—Sara Littlecrow Russell, "Urban Skin,"
from the We Got Issues! Performance Piece

Rha Rants

I was recently pulled over for speeding by a police officer in Jersey. Because I was polite, he knocked down the reported mileage per hour and encouraged me to come to court so I would get less of a fine.

Cultural bulletin: Black people have a real aversion to going to court—yes, even when we know we are not criminals.

I promptly returned home and asked my husband, my white Jewish attorney husband, who gets a cluster of speeding tickets every year, if I should just pay it off. "Here's how it works," he confidently told me. "You'll go in, the police officer will be there, the prosecutor will conference you in the hallway, and they'll offer you a reduced deal. You'll probably pay a fine, but no points and no insurance reporting."

Somehow, even with all his convincing, I could not persuade the pit of my stomach that it would be OK. On the day I'm scheduled to go to court, the trepidation returns. I pout like a little girl and ask my husband if he'll come with me. He laughs, kisses me on my forehead, and sends me out the door with a "Don't worry. If you have a problem, call."

The courtroom and hallway are packed—all races, classes, sizes, languages. The prosecutor arrives, and we get a five-minute rant on how he doesn't even want to hear our excuses. This is not how my husband told me it would go! I am out the door and on the phone. More laughter, and "Don't worry—call me after you see him."

I gravitate toward the other young women, an Italian and an Asian sister. We nervously introduce ourselves and admit our offenses; I was clocked at sixty-eight, the Italian at sixty-five, the Asian, seventy-three.

Over the next ninety minutes I watch in horror and amazement at how America's justice is handed down in traffic court. In descending order, favorable sentences go to: white males with a lawyer; white females with a lawyer; white anyone with a parent; non-white, non-black folks with a lawyer; white males; white females; non-white, non-black people; English-speaking, black females; black males; and those who do not speak English, who get it the worst—with the exception of black males who are in handcuffs.

Here's the most poignant moment: A white businessman with a lawyer in tow is charged with reckless endangerment, driving while under the influence, and resisting arrest for pushing a police officer; the judge tells him he is willing to drop the latter charge, but only if the businessman turns to the police officer and gives a "sincere apology."

You can hear the mouths of all the black folks in the room drop in disbelief as we remember Rodney King. Finally, a brother mumbles under his breath, "Can we all apologize and go home?"

I get a charge of unsafe driving, pay a fine of $155 dollars, and head back over the George Washington Bridge vowing to never speed again. But that's the least of my worries. I cannot shake the incredible inequity I just witnessed and experienced. Justice in this country is purely subjective.

What is even more unsettling is that neither the judge nor the prosecutor was rude, nor did they make any overtly racist remarks. They genuinely appeared like calm, rational professionals, trying to do the best job they could. Were they even aware of what they were doing?

I wanted to march, I wanted to rage, I wanted to stand up in the midst of it all and scream "Can't you see what's happening here?" But the only thing black people have a bigger aversion to than court is jail.

My husband welcomes me home, hugs me, and says how happy he is that I got the charge reduced. I try to tell him about what I witnessed, but he's focused only on what happened to me. As the days go by and I'm pulled deeper and deeper into my own life, I, too, begin to shift my focus back in the same direction.

If I had a nickel for every incident like this, for every offensive joke, gesture, dismissal, detention, or every outrageous injustice experienced by women, people of color, poor people, immigrant people, and conscious compassionate white folks, I would be rich, rich, rich!

It's almost fifty years after the inception of the civil rights movement, and we still have yet to overcome. As a matter of fact, many would argue that when it comes to civil and human rights, the clock is rapidly rolling backwards, thanks to political greed and ambition newly cloaked in the war on terrorism. Even though the "figureheads" have become more culturally diverse, they are perpetuating the same white supremacist, world-domination ideologies that breed hatred, indifference, and fear.

The struggle is no longer black and white; these ideologies have been internalized, and they've caused some of the most horrendous human violations to be played out among people of the same race, gender, and culture. We have become a nation filled with self-hatred and loathing that gets masked with lip gloss and hairspray, then ripped apart for the cameras of primetime reality TV. And somehow, just like that judge and prosecutor in New Jersey, we don't see it. We think it's "normal"—business as usual.

And that is exactly what it is—business. This country has created a pecking order of identity in the name of economic gain and sociopolitical influence. Billions of dollars are spent and even more made by the industrial machine to keep you aspiring, aspiring, *aspiring*.

How much are we as young women talking to one another about race, culture, and class? And not just what we think "the man" is doing to us—what about what we do to ourselves and each other? How many times have I heard young women say, "I just can't be friends with other women?" How many times have *I* said it? How many times have I watched women call each other bitches, threaten physical violence, make fun of differences in language, speech, style of dress, or hair? How many times have I changed the subject when a white girlfriend makes an offensive comment over dinner, or used our friendship as a license to tell me about their black nannies, or how I'm different from those other black girls?

How many "bout it" young activist women who are afraid to confront their own privilege—aka their ignorance—philosophically starve themselves 'cause they say it brings them closer to the people, but won't even take the time to get to know the same sistas they swear they are rescuing and defending? And what makes them think that rescuing and defending is the answer, or that our middle-class elitist judgments that separate the hoodrats and hos from the ones we really should be "saving" solves the problem?

So often, we are encouraged to see ourselves as victims, to justify our behavior by paying lip service to the rhetoric of internalized oppression, but how often do we look each other in the eye and say, "I am struggling with this, and I know it is not who I am."

We've got to be willing to confront our differences, challenge our ignorance, and transform our assumptions about who is the "victim" and who is the "perpetrator." The lines have never been clear, and they're more blurred now than ever before.

WGI! sees this movement as an opportunity to be reborn and forge a new vision of ourselves and our world.

It begins by asking, What are the most valuable aspects of our herstory, and how do we bring those to bear on the state of our world?

What riches have our diverse experiences given us, and how can we use them to celebrate, strengthen, and uplift humanity?

What are the infinite resources that each of us has been endowed with? How can we most effectively share those resources?

This is about *power*—personal, social, and political—and how to achieve and sustain it. The dominant world culture teaches us that there is not enough to go around, and, therefore, some of us must be left out.

It will take great courage to refute this lie. Each of us must be willing to stand in the center of this conversation, not just as allies for one another, but as full and rightful owners of the opportunity to transform a distorted and twisted legacy. Each of us must be willing to look one another in the eye, grab hands, and say, "Let's break free, *together*!"

Tarek Aylouch

Courageous

Suheir Hammad

Suheir Hammad is a poet born to Palestinian parents and raised in Brooklyn, New York. She is the author of Born Palestinian, Born Black *and* Drops of This Story, *as well as her latest poetry collection,* ZaatarDiva. *Suheir is an original writer and cast member of the Tony Award–winning* Russell Simmons Presents Def Poetry Jam on Broadway.

Age:
32
Cultural Identity:
Palestinian American
Born:
In Jordan
Education:
Life
Occupation:
Poet
Economic Class:
Working
Marital Status:
Girl, please
Registered to Vote:
Yeah

❶ When was the first time you noticed you were different?

I grew up in Sunset Park, Brooklyn, during the 1980s. The majority of my neighbors were Puerto Rican, and being Palestinian, I was a minority within a minority. I also grew up in a refugee home, and was often told the story of Palestinian exile. So I always felt a responsibility to the suppressed narratives of my parents and ancestors. Within my family, my goals and dreams were not considered proper for a female.

We were raised as young girls with the responsibility of the household and that was the epitome of what a woman was supposed to do. But the economic reality represented something different. I worked with my father as a child and did not have holidays off. The immigrant work ethic—the ethic of the working poor—cannot afford the luxury of dictating traditional roles. This work ethic is not respected in mainstream society.

I was also different because of my desire to do creative work. I could not find answers to my questions, i.e., why can't a woman be a poet? She has to travel by herself, and she has to meet and work with different cultures and environments. It was very intimidating to consider being a working artist. The public schools did not encourage it. From all angles I was told that this was not attainable for me without a sacrifice I might not be willing or able to endure.

❷ What fuels your activism?

Love. It's a worldview I have. Growing up, I felt apart from my peers in school, and in the artistic community I felt apart. Any time I felt brokenhearted—that is when I felt the most isolation. When I began to look at where I felt the most happy, connected, and inspired, the common thread was the environment of love. I don't want to feel isolated, so I choose to love. I want to feel connected, so I choose to love.

❸ If there is anything you could say to young women about the issues of prejudice, and the work we have to do to overcome this, what would it be?

I would ask the following questions: Do you love yourself? Do you forgive yourself? Are you willing to transform yourself? Do you trust yourself?

The rule is to take a step back to be able to see the larger picture. These questions remind me of who I am. We are told that our income, job, salary, status is who we are, but all of these things are projections that people make money from. The question, Am I willing to be transformed? is not a question society encourages us to ask.

❹ What insights have you gained around how to confront isms?

I've often found myself in situations in which some fool makes some ignorant remark about Palestinians specifically and Arabs in general.

Because I am Palestinian, my nationality is politicized. If I offer one Palestinian narrative that is counter to the mainstream perception, I am also asked to give a Zionist perspective as if I have not been a part of the dominant machine. The people who silence me and challenge my right to expression have grown up under the same machine and the same ignorance and have been confronted with the same fear. Our appetite for authentic dialogue has been dulled. If I do not confront this reality with compassion, I will be letting everyone down.

This is exhausting. I ask, Why must I be the teacher? What I have found is that when I confront with compassion, I am able to make a difference. If I am not silent, individuals now know that they may have to confront new beliefs when they talk to the next person. If I am silent, we will keep repeating the same words and will not be challenged to grow. We must keep our voices raised, but raised with compassion, and it is very difficult as young women to do that.

❺ How does the media affect/influence/perpetrate/eradicate isms in America?

As a poet, I am most concerned with what is not being said in and shown on the media. We focus on the lives of rich and famous people, while true attention is needed in every area of our own lives, from healthcare to day care.

There are different levels of perception. I don't see Native Americans or physically disabled people in the media. Maybe they are sometimes offered as tokens, but they are not really included in for-profit mainstream popular culture. I don't see enough positive images of Arabs or Arab Americans.

If we were living in another time or place all of these questions around ignorance would be moot. There is no reason for the absence of different bodies, complexions, and cultures in the media except that they do not make money for the larger machine.

❻ What is your greatest wish for young women?

I would hope that we as women create a world that is safer for girls to travel in, because traveling is such a critical part of our human growth. We must create those spaces for them. We must do this, we must.

Some of my friends who are Cambodian, Vietnamese, or Laotian have different stories of being carried on their parents' backs through jungles or having narrowly escaped on boats over dark water. They have different stories of growing up in ghetto projects, carrying butterfly knives in their purses, trying to get off the government cheese.
—Kelly Tsai, "Packing"

Excerpt from "Story"

by Vanessa Huang

my mother speaks to me
in collage

I speak back
in kaleidoscope

I speak to grandmother
in Mandarin
through the phone cord

grasping

a girl from Vietnam
unknowingly speaks
colored girl

tears fall
surfacing pain
echoing herstories
of black women and Chicana sister

American billboards don't advertise
colonialism and slavery

the language of American Dream hides
the violence

my mother speaks to me
recently learning of
colored waiting rooms
colored bus seats
and white water

I speak to people caged in women's prisons
in this language
offering cultural ammunition
sharing the shrapnel I have gathered

reenacting the rape
of the land
of the womb
of the heart beat of a people
on city streets
on city bus lines
Scrappy Gook
tagged in graff
perpetual foreigner
I don't take it personally

on city streets
I speak to young buffalo souljas
street scholars and griot-historians in training
stringing rhymes
for civil war, demanding more

my mother
asks me to edit her life
story
names three goals:

honor father
share story
improve English

she writes in Mandarin
translates for me
to edit her life
story

a Real Immigrant Story

to fit
my allegiances

Vanessa Huang *is a second-generation Chinese-American women and radical feminist of color who strives to build a safer and more compassionate world rooted in healthy, vibrant communities where everyone is worth caring for.*

We as women in general need to stand the fuck up and scream in unison, "WE ARE HERE, WE DO EXIST." Maybe we need to start totin' some AKs as a stark contrast to the babies that are wrapped around us. [We need to teach] our younguns the truth about Hip-Hop, mentor them through the elements. Eventually they will right our wrongs and bring it back full circle. —Asia-One, B-girl

Black Bitch

by Nzingha Byrd

Yesterday,
I was called
a black bitch
The insult flew
from his pickup truck window
and stung my ears
His breath burned
hot from black coffee
no cream

Words spilled from his lips
as if they had been
sleeping in his saliva
awaiting an opportunity
And since "nigger"
retired in 2003
his opportunity was me

Had I not been in my right mind
I probably would have
taken the chance
that he thought my existence
consisted of and
wrapped in jeopardy

around his neck
cutting off all breath

But instead
I lowered my eyes
and spoke softly
"Without me, there would be no you"
He squinted
threw his cup out the window
and pulled off
perplexed
Felt but couldn't fathom
the reality

Now, I sleep in his mind
for hours at a time
and whisper
Everything he wants his wife to be
is brought forth by me
So, he hits her
because he hates black people

Now, how transparent is that
When opportunity called black
brings light to everything
you're scared of

Nzingha Byrd is a twenty-four-year-old African woman from Cincinnati.

"I would hope that we as women create a world that is safer for girls to travel in because traveling is such a critical part of our human growth. We must create those spaces for them. Which traditions are harmful to us? Which traditions support us? We can learn this by sharing stories with the other women we encounter as we travel. We must do this, we must." —Suheir Hammad

Being white means you must listen with humility to all that goes on around you, even when, and especially when, you don t understand it.
—Chelsea Michel Gregory, *Beyond the Myths of Whiteness*

Beyond White Privilege

by Jessie Eller-Issacs

I have been thinking hard about what it means to call myself white. I know that in part it means that I have access. It means that I have skin-color privilege and everyday battles that I don't have to fight. For me (but not for all or even most white people) it means that my parents and my grandparents hold or held graduate-level degrees and own or owned cars and homes.

And still, with all that privilege, I find myself in a struggle. Is it a struggle to process my own guilt in being inherently part of the oppressor race, the oppressor class? In part. Is it a struggle to not hate other white people for their ignorance? Sometimes. Is it a struggle against feeling self-satisfied for being a white person who wants to commit her life to undoing racism? Most of the time.

At the high school in Brooklyn where I work, the young people talk about my whiteness. They call me "white girl," with grinning faces. I don't feel antagonized or attacked. Instead, I feel strangely accepted. They trust me to not lash out at their acknowledgment of my participation in the white supremacy that weaves through their lives, which holds them and their families down. They trust me to know that racism is true for me, too.

Other white people and people of color have taught me the proper language to use to talk about race and racism as a white person. Words like "ally," phrases like "inherent racism" and "white privilege." These words and phrases have started to feel dry in my mouth, to look flat on the page. These words do not tell me, or anyone, what it means for white supremacy to operate within me and the world through which I move. These words and phrases do not tell the story of how white supremacy functions in the hearts and lives of white people. Is white supremacy just too ugly to look at, let alone hold? Is there something just too current about it? Too present? You can't put it in the past, in retrospect, or wrap it beyond recognition in guilt. It is white supremacy, it is racism, and it is part of me and my whiteness.

"Yo miss, I heard you was white?" Armando Espinal looks at me out of the corner of his left eye; his flat-brimmed baseball cap and his smile slant in the opposite direction. He is thirteen and we are doing his math homework. "Yes, I am white," I say. He looks at me full in the face. "No, I mean, white for real."

What does this mean, "white for real"? To me it means my family, my community. To him it means a whole mess of other, less loving things, including the gentrifying class who is moving into his neighborhood and upping his family's rent. Our definitions are able to function in the room, to coexist, but then to also move a little, to become malleable, for him and for me. I love this young man, my student. And at this point, he is beginning to love me. This does not mean he is going to leave my classroom loving all white people. And by no means does my love for him expel racism and white supremacy out of my life and my history. But something is expanding here in how whiteness operates in both of our lives. Somehow, over math homework, we are moving toward a deeper investigation of the story white supremacy demands to tell. The story itself is beginning to move.

Jessie Eller-Issacs is a twenty-five-year-old white educator formerly of the Bay Area, who currently resides in Brooklyn. What would it look like for young white women to lead other white people into new territory around how we can work to undo racism? What is beyond white privilege?

rant

Strangers on Train

by Belia Mayeno Saavedra

It is always a relief
to find a seat on the 6
during rush hour.
Except for all the crotches.
At that angle I am surrounded
by a sea of half-zipped flies
cameltoes
rhinestone belt-buckles slung low on narrow young girl hips
spelling out nicknames
that will be forgotten after junior-high graduation.
I am citizen of Crotchlandia
from 68th to 42nd streets.
Mostly—it's OK.
Until
the doors open and
there is a man in the swelling tide of riders
with pocked brown skin
sharp *Indio* cheekbones
a bulging backpack
and sweatpants.
I sheepishly smile to myself and look down at the floor.
Embarrassed for him,
but feeling just a little kinship too.
As far as I can see on this Upper East Side train
only he and I share indigenous roots.

So I figure,
who really cares
if he accidentally, unfortunately, pops a boner
every now and then.
But then he reaches in his pocket and makes a motion
like he is jiggling change
or fidgeting with house keys
and he pushes himself towards the perky designer-jean buttocks
of an oblivious girl.
The prayer changes.
Don't
Don't do it
Don't give them a reason to believe that they were right all along
when they called
our grandfathers
our fathers
our cousins, brothers, *tios,* and friends
filthy
perverts
less than barnyard animals.
Don't.
Don't make me choose
between the unknowing girl with carnation-pink cheeks
and calling you out in front of the huge ham-fisted white man
who looks at you like you are trash.
The Cruz Azul patch on your bag announces
you are a *futbol* fan.
Your scapular for Nuestra Senora de Guadalupe
says you are a believer too.
You are not defined by this moment
of violation and betrayal.
But you should know
that the smiling girl's curvy ass
doesn't define her either.
So I begin with a whisper
No le toques
No le toques, senor.

The train lurches forward
the start/stops give you an excuse to push harder onto the girl
She continues to laugh with her friend.
So I get louder
No le toques
Don't touch her.
Yo te veo
I see you.
I see you
I see you
I see every brown man
who ever lifted my skirt
grabbed my ass
called me bitch
made me feel fucking stupid
for believing that we as Raza
are in this together.
No le toques—Cochino!
Loudest now
Finally you hear me,
nonchalantly back away from the girl
a few steps.
The train stops.
You slip away into the human tangle.
Yo te veo . . .
I see you.
And I am asking you now
my brother
my brothers
I ask you to see me too.

> yo mama so ugly
> she melt mirrors, i say.
> america shrug like
> whatever. yo mama so
> poor i jailed her.
> —Lenelle Möise, "Stripes," from
> the We Got Issues! Performance
> Piece

Belia Mayeno Saavedra *is a twenty-five-year-old Japanese and Chicana woman from Oakland. She was born and raised in CalifAztlan. She learned to love radical politics, art, literature, and poker from her always-inspiring Mayeno family.*

Brother

by Adrienne Maree Brown

Some days the men in my life make me feel like I should forget it all. Any lift-myself-up moment can end up accosted by your gaze or your pushing hands. At night I sit with a "comrade" and we talk about how it all will be can still end up with him on top of me asking me please through a whiskey haze 'cause "the movement is lonely." When do we have that talk about how lonely living is, how loneliness is our misunderstanding of the way earth is our greatest ally, and how much more lonely it becomes when my thoughts on the wounding path of power pursuit is met with your statement of my beauty.

Women, we've always been beautiful, but we've never been free, equal. Where do I cast my ballot against rape and the pressure that precedes it, that pressure when I say I don't think so and you don't leave, where you use your presence and my desire to trust you against me, to wear me down and spread me out and enter me and fuck with my sacredness? Where do I register my rage against the sick dynamic borne when you ask me for my body, as a man—a black man—who I work so constantly to bring closer to me on the ancient cyclical walk toward a better realization of why breath and why thought? You ask me questions I can answer only with rejection.

Where do I mark the page to say I don't want your sex or your heat, I want your soul and your brilliance? Where do I pull the lever that lifts your expectant weight off of me and allows our work to begin? Some days I wake up furious that you slipped into my comfort under the guise of a soldier on my side of the nebulous line and ruined another night of change with your petty, unfocused, unstoppable lust. Why should I care and organize and fight when it's your cold hands grabbing, no great white terror, but those of my beloved, hands that reach out from beside me, not behind me.

What kind of victory can we have when you are so constantly trying to defeat me?

Adrienne Maree Brown is the executive director of the Ruckus Society (www.ruckus.org). She cut her national organizing teeth as cofounder of the League of Young Voters, where she created training and communications programs and coedited How to Get Stupid White Men Out of Office. *Her work focuses on power and pleasure. She is also a writer, singer-songwriter, traveler, and organizational developer.*

Some days, when I walk into the office and people ask me how I'm doing, I want to say, "Pretty fuckin' colonized!" But instead, I say, "I'm fine, how are you?" And I smile. Smile pretty as that chick on the Land O'Lakes box, pretty as the Mazola Corn girl (who was Filipino, by the way), pretty as a crouching mountain lion that's about to rip your throat out. But I can never let them see the angry Indian. Their genes remember that Indians are really bloodthirsty savages and I am safe only if I let them see the little buckskinned Indian maiden holding out a basket of corn for them to wrap their greedy mouths around.
—Sara Littlecrow Russell, "Urban Skin," from the We Got Issues! Performance Piece

Ritual of Empowerment

In 1990, after hearing Bill Bradley state, "If you've never had a conversation about race, you are part of the problem," Wall Street attorney Corey Kupfer began to contemplate his own commitment to improving race relations in this country. "I regularly talked to my friends and colleagues of different races, ethnic backgrounds, and cultures about many intimate subjects, but had I ever had an honest, personal, and totally open conversation about race? No."

Fueled by this realization, Kupfer founded a project called Conversations About Race, which encourages individuals to have intimate, personal, one-on-one conversations about race with someone from another race or culture. As part of our commitment to an empowered movement that includes all young women, WGI! encourages you to have such a conversation. Even if you do not have anyone close to you that fits this description, use this ritual as an opportunity to engage someone outside of your immediate community and or comfort level. Typically, these conversations last for about ninety minutes. However, our experience has been that once people begin the conversation, it's hard to stop! It's important to find a quiet, intimate space where you and your conversation partner will not be disturbed, and to agree ahead of time to the guidelines, which are:

- The conversation is open and honest.
- Any question may be asked, any comment may be made, any

fear may be expressed, and any concern may be communicated.
- The conversation focuses on personal life experiences instead of debated political issues.
- All elements of the conversation will be received as a contribution to each of the participant's lives and understanding of other people.

Sample questions:

- How do you define race?
- Where did you grow up? What was it like for you growing up?
- What incidents or comments have affected you regarding race?
- What do you want people to know about your race?
- What do you want to know that you have been afraid to ask about my race?

We would love to hear about your conversations. Please log onto the website at www.wegotissues.org and share your experience.

We Got Stats!

➡ Victims reported an average of **191,000 hate crime incidents** annually since 2000. —U.S. Department of Justice

➡ **Rates of hate crimes are similar across genders, races, and ethnic groups.** —U.S. Department of Justice

➡ In 2004, the Equal Employment Opportunity Commission received 4,512 reports of **pregnancy-based discrimination**.
—U.S. Equal Employment Opportunity Commission

➡ Approximately **15,000 sexual harassment cases** are brought to the EEOC each year. —Nikki V. Katz. About.com

➡ **Overweight and obese women have lower incomes** ($6,700 a year less) and higher rates of poverty (10% higher) than their non-obese peers. —National Organization for Women Foundation

➡ As of March 2001, the majority of women in the workplace were still in **traditional "female" occupations**, e.g., 79% of administrative support workers were female. —U.S. Census Bureau

➡ Women are at a higher risk for **housing discrimination** due to their overwhelming status as **domestic violence victims and immigrant domestic workers.** —American Civil Liberties Union (2005)

➨ Although the issue of **gender persecution** came into the global consciousness in the 1990s, U.S. borders remain largely closed to black and brown women seeking gender asylum. Gender is not listed as a category for asylum eligibility. —Women's Institute for Leadership Development for Human Rights

➨ In 1971, Nixon vetoed a Comprehensive Child Development Act that **would have made child care available to all children** at a cost of $2 billion; subsequent child care bills failed. —Jennifer Roesch, Socialist Worker Online (2004)

Chapter 4

Hot Stuff!
Sex, You, and Reality

Women who stand complete in their power make me wet
In the head
In the eyes
In the heart.

—StaceyAnn Chin, "Afrodesiac," from the We Got Issues!
Performance Piece

Jlove Rants

Like many women, I learned from a very young age that my body was
a tool to get what I wanted, from devoted attention to lustful affection. I was in control, determined to find and keep love the best way I
knew how. I often felt a surge of power when I manipulated men with
my beauty, charm, and wit. It came so easily to me that it became part
of my personality.

It didn't start out this way, of course. In the beginning, it was
the older boys teaching me and my girlpals how to play Doctor, which
graduated to Spin the Bottle and I'll Show You If You Show Me. At the

time, I didn't think there was anything wrong with these games. I mean, sure, the older boys told us it was a secret—but that was part of the fun. Anyway, these were boys I trusted, looked up to, and loved. I didn't think that they would possibly harm me or my friends. But I was wrong.

I don't necessarily blame any of those boys. They must have learned it somewhere; they were probably doing what someone else had done to them. And, come on, how many people haven't played Doctor? But the result of our playtime was that I was a highly sexualized young being, still just a child, who didn't understand the complexities of it all. What I did know, though, is that boys liked it, and therefore they liked *me*. Wrong there, too.

Much of my adolescent life was spent making the same mistakes over and over again. I thought the way to a guy's heart was through my body. In college, after a couple of psychology and women's studies classes, coupled with failed romances, I figured out that the answer didn't lie between my legs. Just as I was beginning to change my ways, I survived a date rape attempt. That got my attention! In the aftermath, I realized that I was looking for someone to love me. I remember scribbling madly in my journal, "love me love me love me lovemelovemelovemelove meloveme meloveme?"

Me love me?

Finally, at the age of twenty-three, I understood what had gotten in the way of my happiness. And with that clarity came liberation. After a brief bout of depression where I was questioning my perceptions and beliefs about sexuality, and slowly, carefully I began weaving, creating, and loving my own new reality.

And now, I am right.

Now, I enjoy being sexy without the need to use my sexuality to get what I want. I've learned to have platonic relationships where my goal isn't to get another person to want me, and I've let go of childhood transgressions. I've worked out forgiving myself for who I used to be.

I have healed.

We Got Issues! spontaneous excercise: Where are *you* around sex and sexuality? Will you tell us? I am (check as many as you want):

A. Enjoying mind-blowing, guilt-free, multiorgasmic sex.
B. Having it, but it's definitely not mind-blowing.
C. Happily and unapologetically abstinent.

D.   Somewhere between A and B, depending on the night.

E.   Underserved and in need of sexual healing—fast.

We wanna know.

Despite the fact that mainstream media still holds up size-zero as the hallmark of beauty, we know who the real divas are. And size zero just can't fit, 'cause we got too much to hold.

So, would the sexually liberated, spiritually grounded, emotionally healthy young women of the world please stand up? We know you (we) are out there! Whatever your reality is, we know there's no "one size fits all" model of beauty, nor any reactionary political initiative that can define us or our sexuality. We define who we are in this world, and when the shoe doesn't fit, well, we just go out and buy a new pair.

Laws and social norms will come and go, but when you look at our changing herstory, one thing remains constant—there have always been women who said, "Oh, hell no!" to sexual oppression. And boy, haven't the boys been busy: From chastity belts to marriage knots to potshots at Roe v. Wade, the Bush administration and its right-wing allies are determined to control women's sexuality.

So where are we now, we post-hippie, Hip-Hop, shop-'till-the-sale-stops young women who have been raised in this era of chick lit and third-wave feminism? We've witnessed Ellen coming out on national TV and the government denouncing same-sex marriage. We've experienced the rise of raunch culture and its icons, like Paris Hilton. Cake sex parties—which bill themselves as "feminism in action"—Internet porn, and live sex podcasting invite our generation's answers to the question: What does sexual liberation *really* look like?

Are we:

Embracing our sexy?

Loving our bodies as our temples?

Defining our sexual spirits as we see fit?

Joyfully masturbating in the mirror 'cause we so fine?

When you are alone, with you and your truth, do you feel sexily realized?

We wanna know.

Vanessa Vargas

Bold

Lenelle Moïse

Age:
26
Cultural Identity:
Haitian American
Born In:
Port-au-Prince, Haiti
Education:
MFA in playwriting from
Smith College, BA from
Ithaca College
Occupation:
Poet, playwright, perform-
ance artist, interdisciplinary
risk-taker
Economic Status:
Economically poor
Marital Status:
Domestic partnership
Registered to vote:
N/A

Lenelle Moïse (www.lenellemoise.com) is a Haitian-American feminist poet, playwright, and Drammy-winning performance artist. She cowrote the feature film Sexual Dependency *(2003) and has served as resident playwright for the Drama Studio* (Little Griot, 2006), *the Next Wave of Women in Power* (We Got Issues!, 2004) *and the Kitchen Theatre Company* (Purple, 2001). *Her prose appears in* Red Light *(Arsenal Pulp Press) and* Homewrecker *(Soft Skull Press). Lenelle is a member of the Chrysalis Theatre Ensemble. She facilitated Planned Parenthood's* I Am . . . Renaming the Sexual Revolution, *a spoken-word CD, and series of "slam poetry meets sex ed" workshops. She is the author of a forthcoming audio poetry collection,* Madivinez, *and is currently touring her "autobiofictional" one-woman show,* WOMB-WORDS, THIRSTING.

❶ When was the first time you discovered you were sexual?

I was an avid reader. At age ten, I snuck my mother's copy of Alice Walker's *The Color Purple* off the shelf and have read it at least fifteen times since. The woman-love and masturbation explored in the text weren't so much a revelation, but an affirmation of my sexuality. By then, I had already discovered the intense joy of having a clitoris, and I had already "played house" with neighborhood girlfriends. But seeing those urges documented in Walker's novel affirmed that I wasn't a deviant. Out there somewhere, there were other brown-skinned women-love women touching themselves without guilt.

❷ How do you define sexuality?

Sexuality is a vehicle for realizing freedom. Sexuality is an opportunity to expand/break the boxes and boundaries of our imaginations.

❸ How did your upbringing influence your sexuality?

My mother always invited me into the kitchen when she was making meals with her women friends. In the absence of their male partners, the women spoke often and frankly about (heterosexual) sex. There were funny anecdotes, there were cautionary tales. I remember hearing about a woman in Haiti who made herself very sick soaking her vagina with cleaning agents for a whole month before she got married. She hoped to make her vagina stiff and tight for her wedding night so that her husband's penetration would make her bleed. She wanted to fool him into believing he was her first and only lover. This story has two morals: 1) You should be a virgin when you get married. 2) If you aren't a virgin when you get married, don't stupidly hurt yourself pretending that you are.

❹ What fuels your work around your sexuality?

Pleasure is our birthright. We shouldn't be hindered from or punished for pursuing it. I want everyone to feel free to express their sexuality; not just in their bedrooms, but in casual conversation, in their screenplays and e-mails.

❺ What turns you on?

I'm turned on by deep thinkers. I love to interrupt a passionate political debate with a passionate kiss. I love to be whispered to. I love to be called by name. I love when sexual intimacy feels spontaneous and urgent—like *if we don't make love right now, the sun won't come out tomorrow.*

❻ How does your sexuality impact your life?

I try to start "from the bottom up" in my quest for an evolved consciousness. I am very inspired by Audre Lorde's essay "Uses of the Erotic," which reminds us to act viscerally—to act from our pelvis—not just in the bedroom but in every aspect of our everyday lives. We must learn to trust the signals sent from those parts of ourselves closest to the earth.

❼ What does a sexually empowered young woman look like?

She struts shamelessly. She dances like no one's watching. She winks often. She smiles only when she means it. Her mouth seems ready to speak or to sigh or to moan at her whim.

❽ Is the conversation of sexuality personal or political?

Both. Until we live in a society where people are free to love themselves and each other without state-sanctioned prevention or intervention, we cannot afford to keep our sex lives to ourselves. I recite Audre Lorde's mantra, "Your silence will not protect you," like, everyday, 'cause if we stay quiet, we render ourselves invisible; and if we are invisible, the perpetuators of the imperialist hypercapitalist patriarchy will walk right through us.

❾ How are sexuality and spirituality connected?

Our culture really tries to separate mind from matter and body from soul, but the two go hand in hand. Would God give you the glorious ability to come if It didn't welcome your coming? To paraphrase Shug Avery: It pisses God off if you walk by beautiful trees and don't notice them. I say, we women need to climb the trees of our sexualities. We need to carve our names into the bark. We need to take naps in the shade. We need to pick and eat fruit hanging from the branches. We need to plant more seeds and watch our self-love grow.

❿ Why is sex so taboo for us as young women?

Let's face it, sex is taboo for everyone! In fact, I think the Internet porn industry relies on our collective secrecy about sex and sexuality; people pay big bucks to view the taboo. Wouldn't it be cheaper to discuss so-called scandalous acts with our lovers and friends? Repression is the midpoint between implosion and explosion. On the other hand, curiosity may have killed the cat, but it won't kill the pussy, ya'll!

I look around me and
see pregnant girls with
children, and bills, and
stress, and no pearls.
—Maya Acevedo,
Mexican/Boricua student

Beautiful

by Girlstory

We live to see ourselves
every day,

mirror to
face,

we criticize the
pimples,

the wrinkles,
who we are.

I can't wash away the future and put the past to sleep.
This thing haunts me at night.
With my head to the wall

close enough to kill myself with the wrong move.

I wish I could.
I was never afraid of change,
the mirror told me lies but I never
listened.

I wasn't afraid to lock my door that night,
to play the music low.

This skin isn't my own
and I'm trying to get out,
feel myself out,

let it all out.

Lying naked in bed.

At night.
When no one is watching
I could pretend
I was someone else.
I'd be pretty the way all the boys wished I was.
I'd be popular and smart the way my parents wished I was.
I wouldn't feel weird about my body,
or the way it bled
or the way I wanted sex.
I wouldn't feel desire trapped in my throat
with nowhere to go.

Makeup would be the key,
but I doubt that I am a made-up person.

What am I afraid of?
I got to be up front with who I am.
These stretch marks and bruises
my body has bared with pride.

I can't hide under clothes forever,
let my body be what it is,

nature between my thighs,

all is beautiful because I gave birth to it,
so forget all of you who distrust
my age or
my size,

the length of what God blessed me.
I feel the need to be dancing
in my size-ten shoes.

I am not scared of
swaying hips
and scars.

I'm not afraid of
drooping breasts.

I'm scared of losing what
it feels like to be just

enough.

I'm afraid of forgetting
what it's like to be

beautiful.

Girlstory is a multigenerational, multicultural women's performance poetry collective based in New York City. Its members range in age from fifteen to thirty-five, and are from Puerto Rico, India, Jamaica, the Philippines, Alaska, Chicago, Seattle, Kentucky, and New York City.

Just because it bucks beneath your touch
And just because I wrap my legs around your hips
Don't think I believe the stories spun by your lips.
—Lisa Ascalon, "I'm a Big Girl"

When people create, they want to defy God. I understand transsexuality in that way.
—Adriana, Kenia's cousin

A Woman in the Making

by Kenia Vazquez

A transsexual is a constructed woman; for me, she is not a man, but a human being who constructs her gender—a woman who decides to create herself.

> —Adrianna, Kenia's cousin

I am Kenia Vazquez.

Yo soy Kenia Vazquez.

When I introduce myself, I just say I'm Kenia. It's like you introducing yourself and saying "Hi, I'm straight."

I used to consider myself a straight guy because my family is old-fashioned. They always talked bad about gays. They always let me know that being gay was the wrong thing. So I would fight with myself to not be gay. I tried to live like I was straight. I never let anybody know my feelings until I was sixteen years old. Then I accepted myself—I lived two years as a gay boy, and then I could see that everybody would confuse me with a woman. So I decided to live as a woman.

I had to leave my house when I was eighteen years old. I told my family I was leaving on vacation and that I was not coming back, because I wanted to live as a woman. They said that it was OK: Whatever I decided to do with my life, they loved me and just wanted me to be happy. The first time I went back it was as a woman with a boyfriend, and in a dress and everything.

When I was twenty-three years old I was working as a topless dancer in Mexico, and I got addicted to crystal. My best friend knew about my addiction. He knew a girl in New York who was a madame, so I went to New York and started working for her. For the first time in my life I had a lot of money in my hands. I could buy everything I wanted. But it was very bad, because I had to go to bed with fat people, with old people, with all kinds of people. I had to go to bed with people I didn't feel comfortable with.

Here in New York, they talk about freedom, and that gay boys have a very nice time, but they don't really accept us. People are scared of transsexuals, but they have to accept that we are here. I'd like to let people know that we do prostitution because we feel we cannot do anything else. A lot of people have ideas about the way they'd like to work, but they don't think they can do it, so they go into prostitution.

I just want to be listened to like everybody; I am human like everybody, and I just want to be accepted.

I want to see myself at thirty-five years old and a woman—educated, speaking good English. I want to have my own house, my own business, very far away from prostitution; I want to be a productive person.

My happiness would be to feel free—from drugs, prostitution, everything. My happiness would be to feel love—somebody to love me, and to love myself. That would be happiness for me.

When my culture, my society, my mother didn't have any more to teach me, I've learned from Kenia and other transsexuals how to be a human being and how to be a better woman.

> —Adrianna, Kenia's cousin

Kenia Vazquez *is a transsexual prostitute from Mexico currently residing in New York City.*

The Menarche Party

by Megan Andelloux

My thirteen-year-old niece asked me, "Why should I be proud of the fact that I got my period when all these pads offer 'Shh...quiet wrappers'?" Her question dumbfounded me. For years, I had been grooming her for menstruation. As a sex educator, I had the silicone models to teach her anatomy, books to talk about the changes puberty brings, and, most important, I had the pure idealism to fashion a woman who would be proud of her body's cycle. I couldn't let them forge another consumer mortified by her own menstruation! But how could I make my niece proud of her period if the public discourse only involves euphemisms and silence? "Screw the wrappers," I said. "I'm going to throw you a party to celebrate, and to show why you should be happy you menstruate."

So I did.

I got the idea from Inga Muscio's book *Cunt*. Thus was born The Menarche Party. We used lavender- and chamomile-scented panty-liners as nametags. Vulva puppets and tampons dipped in red paint hung from the ceiling. We gave out research papers on the link between tampons and endometriosis, and T-shirts, and buttons. Decorating the walls were 350 euphemisms for menstruation, and 1930s-era hygiene products and vintage vibrators were used as centerpieces. By the end of the night, premenarche girls and currently menstruating women were comparing vulva pictures and oohing over classic '50s menstruation films. One hundred and fifty women, six states, word of mouth, and curiosity: That's what brought them. They all wanted, on some small level, to throw off their shame.

And so now each year I take The Menarche Party on the road to colleges and women's centers. I'm getting through to more and more women every year. And my niece, well, she's become a crusader herself. Proudly wearing her vulva necklace to school, she's unafraid to correct the gym teacher during health class: "No, ma'am, you're able to urinate even with a tampon in." Now if we can just get rid of those "Shh!" wrappers . . .

Megan Andelloux is a twenty-nine-year-old white sex educator who works throughout New England teaching people of all ages about sexuality, relationships, and sex toys; she is the creator of The Menarche Party, a traveling educational party focusing on menstruation, menstrual activism, menstrual health, and attitudes. Visit her at fierecefemmevixens.com

The big question is, what is for sale? And what can make the most money . . . young women are taught that we have to wear skimpy clothes and sell our bodies so we take in that this is what we need to do. Young women will aspire to that no matter what else they are doing in their lives. Think about the stripper pole classes at Crunch!!! —Suheir Hammad

While Janet fantasized about seducing and
being seduced, she surmised that nothing
would come of either because of an obvious and
not-so-obvious fact—the bane of her romantic
[non] existence. She was fat, and a virgin.
—Adona El-Murr, "Janet's Romantic [Non] Existence"

A Virgin

by Una Osato

I had a gyno once who wouldn't look inside me cause she found out I
    was a virgin,
"A virgin—
Well I've never done this to a virgin, a virgin, a virgin—"
Rubbing it in my twenty-year-old face
I was like, enough already, I get it!
Really, it just freaked *her* out—
She sent me away,
Said she didn't feel comfortable sticking that metal rod up my pussy
Wouldn't do the examination because she didn't want me to think of
    that as my first sexual experience—
Why, I would no longer be *a virgin*.
I didn't even get to say a single word.
Like that I was far from a virgin,
I had stuck many other objects up there
I had had sex with fingers and tongues and vibrators and bananas—
My virginity was only without a penis,
I'm a woman of color
Done been fucked over
Been violated already.

I rarely feel comfortable sexually when I hook up with people,
    guys mostly

Cause it's the same thing every time,
A race to stick your dick inside me.
I can feel your penis pushing at my vaginal opening
So I politely shift my pelvis away
Not wanting to have a confrontation
But you find a way back there
And I forget—
People don't talk about sex 'til it's done
But I open my mouth
"I just want to let you know, I'm not gonna have sex with you"
You ask
"Well, why not?"
And I always feel obligated to explain myself,
Just "no" isn't enough.
"It's not just that I don't want to have sex with you, it's that I've
      never had sex with a boy before"
Go ahead, say all the things you think you're supposed to,
"Oh that's cool, I respect you and your decision" he says,
But a minute ago he was questioning why.

Wish I could explain
I'm not waiting 'til marriage
Just haven't found a boy I'm comfortable enough with to have it,
Kinda simple and boring.

For so long I thought you should be in love,
Now, I just wanna feel comfortable and safe—
Pretty crazy how difficult just that is to find,
Cause I'm twenty-three
And still looking . . .

Una Osato is a twenty-three-year-old Japanese and Jewish woman who currently lives in New York City working as a performer (with her one-women show Keep It Movin'), educator, and babysitter. Since writing this rant, she has had sex with a boy, and it was orgasmically wonderful!

Masaje~Ceremonia

by Gaby Erandi

your fingers draw the map
upon my back

palms dig deep into
the texture of my flesh

beginning at my roots
exploring the terrain
straddling the train tracks
of my spine—
you trace the scars
measure the pain
press your heart against the brownness of my skin
where memories of lack of love remain

the bodypath lays out the journey—
our colonized Mexi'ca hearts
unwind
longing to find
that distant place
transcending space
where dual spirits intertwine
beyond our disillusioned dreams
beyond our sense of time

beyond the leisure of mere sex
we spread
together

the journey now begins
mis cantos
tu placer
the sounds of your desire
transform into a chant:
for love
for life
rising with the smoke of the *copal*

our spirits dance
climaxing into love
we reach
Omecihuatl

La ceremonia
comes full circle
Our souls embrace
I breathe
you sigh
       Respire.

*A twenty-five-year-old Native American and Latina poet, **Gaby Erandi** was born in Michoacan, Mexico, and raised along the migrant farm worker trails of California, Oregon, and Washington State. She currently studies American Indian youth identity development by analyzing Native participation in urban performance poetry such as Hip-Hop and spoken word.*

untitled

by Jennifer Cendaña Armas

at 1:30 a.m.
i'm missing you
in my t-shirt and the violet panties you love
the ones you took off with your teeth the night after we flew into
Bahia
my lights are turned down low
in heavy breaths
i ask if you're by yourself

an index finger
tracing my skin

my finger
discovering the folds of my elbow
to my right temple
gentle
wait to crawl below

your tongue would lead the way if you were here
between my thighs
hands massaging my breasts
but i'm doing ok with your voice
whispering on the phone
as you're touching yourself, too

i would love to kiss you
deep into trance
the musty smells of a hard day's work
caught between our belly buttons
pressed between the palms of our hands against the wall
legs spread apart
wrapping each other close
bite your neck
lick my lips
a tease a minute longer
we
can
come
to
gether

my lover
spiced lust divine
do your kisses travel so quickly to my hips
and how i know you/inside me
even these thousands of miles apart

Jennifer Cendaña Armas *is a multiethnic, multiracial, self-loving, bal-anced supastar creator from Corona/Jackson Heights, Queens, forever traveling the world.*

I overtook you, disarmed you
with my weapons of mass seduction
used each one to tactically blow your mind
You were lost and confused
with nowhere to hide.
—Angela Hardison, "Make Love, Not War?"

Ritual of Empowerment

This ritual breaks down the old to create the new with a two-part exercise using journaling and meditation. First, explore the following questions in your journal:

- What is your highest vision of your sexuality?
- What makes you feel sexy?
- When you think of your sexuality, where do you feel the most expressed? The least?
- In what ways do you feel most connected to your sexuality?
- Is there anything in the way of you being fully sexually expressed? If so, what would it take to work through the barriers? Are you willing to do that?

Next, do a lying mediation:

Find a comfortable room and lie down on your back. You can have your eyes open or closed. Begin to relax your body and your mind. You may want to stretch your body in order to get really comfortable.

Visualize how you look from above: your facial features, on down to your torso, your arms, your stomach, and your legs, feet, and toes.

Acknowledge how much your body does for you every day, on demand; take some time to give thanks to your body for supporting you. Next, acknowledge your strengths, all the contributions you make to this world, and your unique perspective on life.

Explore your image of yourself as a sexual being. Think about what you wrote in your journal, and let those ideas begin to live in your body.

Notice how your body responds when you think about being sexually expressed.

Picture a glorious sexual thought or experience. Pay particular attention to your emotions, without judging. Stay with this experience, and the feelings and emotions that it evokes, until it is complete for you.

Now, think of your highest vision that you journaled about. Inhale and exhale deeply. Picture yourself fully sexually expressed. Inhale and exhale. Slowly, with that image in mind, bring yourself back to the room. For the rest of the day, your mantra is: I deserve to be sexually expressed.

Here are some other rituals you can use to engage your sensuality and sexuality:

- List the top ten reasons why you are sexy. Share them with ten friends.
- Set some sacred time aside and take a bubble bath: Set up candles, incense, and essential oils; put on relaxing music.
- Love your body through healing touch; go out and get a massage or enlist a friend to give you one at home.
- Buy yourself a vibrator and make love to yourself.
- Create an altar to honor your sexuality; have different elements on your altar, such as candles, a small bowel of water, flowers, or anything else you feel belongs there.
- Say this mantra to yourself every day (or make one up that you love): I love myself. I am perfectly healthy and radiantly beautiful.

We Got Stats!

➡ About one fourth (17) respondents believed that a woman or a man who engaged in oral sex with an opposite-sex partner would lose her or his virginity . . . More respondents (56%) thought that anal intercourse between a man and woman could **constitute virginity loss.**
—Laura M. Carpenter, The Journal of Sex Research (2001)

➡ Defining virginity loss to include same-sex encounters implies an understanding of 'real' sex that **challenges heterosexist norms.** —Laura M. Carpenter, The Journal of Sex Research (2001)

➡ **By challenging traditional definitions of virginity loss,** individuals and social groups can help alter prevailing criteria for assigning social identity and possibly promote **greater social equality.**
—Laura M. Carpenter, The Journal of Sex Research (2001)

➡ 50% of females between 15 and 19 are nonvirginal, and **almost 80% of teenagers have experienced sexual intercourse by age 18.**
—E. O. Laumann, J. H. Gagnon, R. T. Michael, and S. Michaels, The Social Organization of Sexuality: Sexual Practices in the United States (1994); Ira L. Reiss with Harriet M. Reiss, Solving America's Sexual Crises (1997)

➡ Many young adults are at great risk of infection with **sexually transmitted diseases (STDs)** because they possess a **false sense of invulnerability**, have more than one sexual partner, are covert about sexual behavior, and lack appropriate and detailed sexual information.
—Ira L. Reiss with Harriet M. Reiss, Solving America's Sexual Crises (1997)

➡ **63% of STDs in the United States occur in people younger than 25 years of age.**

—Ehrhardt, Yingling, and Warner, Annual Review of Sex Research (1991)

Chapter 5

Who You Rollin' With?
Divas Need Love Too

Let there be no purpose in friendship save the deepening of the Spirit.
—Kahlil Gibran

JLove Rants

Life is nothing but a series of relationships. No matter how you slice it, our state of being in the world has everything to do with 'em: from your wisdom-filled Nana to your partner who simultaneously drives you up the wall *and* knows the depth of your soul as no one else does.

The fundamental questions to ask yourself are: How do you find (and keep) healthy, balanced, loving, nourishing, and fun relationships in your life? How do you nurture those people who help make you whole? How do you learn to avoid the people who take your power, drain you, and make you feel less-than? And what about your relationship with yourself—what state is that one in?

Fortunately, I am surrounded by a powerful circle of sisters across the country, from Colorado to California to New York, who give me love, support, late-night talks, laughter, and the occasional kick in the ass. We don't like to see each other messing up or settling for less than we deserve, so we do what we gotta do: interventions. Yes, I've planned many for my homegirls, as well as endured some—from abusive boyfriends and addiction to sorting out our feelings around what our rightful path is in this world, it feels like we've seen and dealt with it all! Communication has always been the cornerstone of our sistercircle. And ladies, lemme tell you, that has not always been an easy one for me!

One of the first training and development sessions that I took with Rha Goddess was called "Fierce Conversations." She asked, "What are the conversations you have been unable or unwilling to have, that if you were able to have, might have changed everything?" She instructed us to make a list of the people, the outstanding issues, and how long overdue the conversations were.

Mine was exhaustively long, and, not surprisingly, included just about every special person in my life. The worst part, though, was the number of years I had been avoiding certain conversations. The longest one was ten years: Ten years of *not* speaking my truth to someone whom I obviously love and who obviously loves me. What was I so afraid to confront?

I got in touch with my attachment to the outcome of the conversation— my fear of what might happen if I said those words and confronted those feelings. I worried that the friendship would end in one of those bitter divorces, where your other friends have to choose sides and you don't get invited to the same parties, blah blah blah, we've seen it all before.

But, like many things that seem so scary and insurmountable, when I gathered enough courage to put my authentic self on the line and say what I needed to say, what came back—after a long, difficult discussion with my friend—was understanding, and then, after a while, healing. Now that friendship is stronger than ever, and we talk more easily about the hard things.

You don't always have control over who you have relationships with— you're born with your family, and you've gotta deal with coworkers, bosses, teachers, and neighbors whether you like them or not. But you get to pick the rest of the people in your life.

It's time for us all to get our own tribes in order; it's time to gracefully let go of those relationships that no longer serve us, and to embrace those that do. It is time for us to embrace ourselves, again or for the very first time.

Each relationship in your life right now has something to teach you. Are you open to the lesson?

Empowered

Aya de León

Age:

38

Cultural Identity:

Black and Latina

Born:

In California

Education:

BA, some grad school

Occupation:

Artist

Economic Class:

Raised working/middle

Marital Status:

Married

Registered to vote:

Democrat/Green

Writer/performer Aya de León lives in the Oakland Bay Area. Her work has received acclaim in the Village Voice, *the* Washington Post, American Theatre Magazine, *the* Oakland Tribune, *and the* San Francisco Chronicle. *Her award-winning 2004 show, "Thieves in the Temple: The Reclaiming of Hip-Hop," toured with the Hip Hop Theater All Stars. Aya has been a professor at Stanford University and a slam poetry champion. She is currently working on her first novel, a collection of essays about self-love, and is the Wellness Coordinator for Youth Speaks in San Francisco. She has released two spoken word CDs. Visit her at www.ayadeleon.com.*

❶ How did come to love yourself, and how do you sustain that love?

I am an unashamed therapy-head. I've done it all, I promote it all, I believe in it all: therapy, personal-growth workshops, support groups, twelve-step programs, reevaluation counseling, breath work, somatic work, body work, Buddhist meditation, Afro-Christianity, indigenous African religion, prayer partners, mentorship, self-help books. I got a lot out of it, and I still use many of these tools on a daily basis.

Love is an active verb, and I have many loving tools to use in the service of loving myself.

❷ What are your feelings about relationship?

I was celibate [not having sex by choice] for many years in my twenties when I was doing a lot of intensive healing work. Everything pushed my buttons: dating, movies, romantic songs on the radio. I just needed to focus on healing and loving myself. These were awesome years, years when my energy went into myself and my art and my life and my liberation. Sexual relationships are land mines for many of us. For me, having experienced childhood abandonment by my father, sexual abuse outside the family, and lots of isolation and disconnection, sexual and romantic relationships really push my buttons. I needed to have a much stronger sense of myself before I got into another relationship, so I wouldn't lose myself. Also, I needed to develop a strong community of healthy friends that I could count on, so I wouldn't be desperate for a partner to meet my emotional needs.

During my time of celibacy, I married myself—I had a wedding and everything. I wanted to remember that even without a partner, I am whole.

Being "alone" is actually about learning that I am not alone just because I don't have a romantic partner. It's about learning how to be really close to my friends: like sleepover close, like fall on each other and cry close, like call each other late at night or early in the morning cause we feel bad about ourselves close, like snuggle up and watch a DVD close, like learning to give and receive help in the places where our lives get hard close.

As women, we are taught to organize our lives around that *one* relationship. It is supposed to be romantic, heterosexual, and culminate in marriage. Ironically, statistics show that single women score higher on happiness indexes than married women, so the model is a sham. Single women depend more on a larger community of people, and I believe that's how we thrive as humans.

❸ What roles do relationships play in your life now?

People are complicated and have many relationship needs. Early in my healing process, all my friendships were about us getting together and talking about hard stuff in our lives: abuse, addiction, trauma, boundaries, choices, and problem solving.

Nowadays, my life is in much better shape, and I am developing stronger boundaries between healing and social relationships. I am pushing for my relationships with my friends to focus more on fun and joy, and less on processing what's hard in our lives. Part of being a good friend is to get specialized help when we need it, and not to drain our friendships when we need more support than the friendship can provide.

❹ How do you maintain healthy and loving relationships?

So I found this great guy. He's loving, smart, attractive, emotionally available, funny, loyal, quirky, interesting, and sweet: everything I've ever wanted. And guess what? Having a good relationship hasn't really solved any of my problems, except wondering who my partner would be. I still have depressed days, lonely days, stressed days, anxious days. I still need my support system, more than ever. And even though it's a good relationship, we have challenges as a couple, and we get lots of help: couples counseling, peer counseling, etc. Being in a relationship, particularly as a black woman with a black man, just means that we are each bringing our own land mines to the relationship. One of the ways we find them is when we step on them and they blow up. It has been important to bring in other people with better mine-detection skills, and the occasional medic. And even though it's hard, I love my man, and it's a miracle to heal together.

❺ What are the messages we get from society about having a relationship with ourselves?

I really don't like the way that notions of "self-esteem" are being used with young women these days. Much of the talk about women with "low self-esteem" sounds blaming, as if women who are struggling with valuing ourselves are somehow weak or deficient. Women are not valued in this society, are attacked, objectified, traumatized, and exploited. So of course it's difficult to value ourselves. These experiences install little land mines of self-hate, self-doubt, self-sabotage, and self-destruction.

❻ What is the greatest lesson that our relationships can teach us?

The thing I am working on these days is learning how to play more. I spent the past sixteen years working hard to get my life in a good place, and now the goal is to enjoy it. I find myself sometimes waiting for my man to come out dancing with me, or to cultural events, or to the movies. But I can't wait for him. I have to remember that I was single for years, and I learned to depend on my community for fun. I have a thriving career in the arts, I'm writing a novel about young black women healing themselves and finally getting to the good part of the writing process, I just got married to a fabulous partner, I have a great relationship with my mom (after a few years of family therapy!) and my younger sister, and I have amazing friends. I have a great house and am learning to make it a sacred home. My life is going well. Time to dance, play, be close, enjoy!

Options (or, Your Vote Counts)

by Rudy

I fought with Kevin last night. We fought on Wednesday, too. Kevin is a real go-getter. He likes to put 150 percent effort into everything; he likes to plan everyone's schedules. It annoys the shit out of me, because a part of me is very go-with-the-flow, so I get exhausted, and another part of me likes to be the one that plans things, so I feel like he's invading my space. He never picks up his cell phone, he makes promises he can't keep, and he hides things from me if he thinks I won't like them. I believe all men need to be trained, but I'm twenty-seven and I don't want to do any more training.

Kevin fights a nasty fight. He is as proud and fiery as me. But then he also says things like, "I love you. I am trying so hard to make you happy. Isn't that enough?"

He asked me if I've ever been happy in a relationship before, so I counted backwards. In many ways I was happy with Tom, Afua, Dewface, and Karen. But they irked me in as many ways as Kevin does, and even though they loved me very much, that was apparently not enough, because I'm not with them today.

Which makes me wonder—am I inherently incapable of happiness in a romantic relationship?

Maybe for some women, having a good-looking man who makes lots of money and loves her unconditionally is enough. But for me, there's a different checklist to fulfill.

Does he make me feel beautiful?

Does he make me feel safe?

Does he make me feel free?

Does he know how to protect me from myself when I'm hurt, scared, or angry?

Does he know where all my buttons are, and does he know to always push the right ones and never push the wrong ones?

Kevin has a good heart, he's great in bed, my friends love him, and he's always trying to make me smile. I shouldn't be complaining. So why is that all I do?

Option 1—"He's good for now": This is a good opportunity for me to practice patience and appreciate the inherent goodness in others.

Option 2—"A relationship takes work": Even if Kevin doesn't seem like "the one" now, he could become "the one" with time and effort.

Option 3—"He's not good for me": Break up and split our assets.

Option 4—"I am insatiable": Nobody will ever make me happy.

Please cast your vote.

Rudy has no major complaints about life. She lives in San Francisco.

A Daughter's *Man*-ual

by Aleeka Kay Edwards

Yesterday I witnessed the cornerstone in a procession of emotional outbursts that are sure to accompany my father in his old age—I saw him cry for the first time.

My relationship with my father—It's not the sound of my voice. It's my personality, he says—has always been dramatic. However, I am usually the one engaging in the said ocular activity. (Call it a fancy name and it makes me sound tougher.) He never cries, he mostly yells. "Sorry that I keep saying sorry," he once said to me. I understood. His actions usually affirm his love for me. I can always depend on him. He is my protector. He is my heart. But then there are those days when things go awry, he loses his composure, and I am forced to revise the past to justify the present. It would be very easy for me to call a man "evil." He hits . . . you bleed. But I try to understand the growth of that anger seed, probably planted years ago; deep roots appear as red veins in his eyes, too inarticulate to explain his pain, and too self-absorbed to see the pain he causes others. I have always liked subcategories. What's beneath a title is more important to me.

So what could make such a stoic man cry? Did he suddenly connect with the beauty of the earth? Unfurrow his brow? Find peace with God and himself? No, dear reader. He was watching *American Idol*. A seventeen-year-old girl was singing Billie Holiday in the sweetest coloratura soprano peppered with trills that brought my father to tears. I would have cried too—but I was PMSing. I have no idea what his excuse is.

Musicians like to criticize *American Idol* because they claim its karaoke qualities mock the struggle of real musicians. I like *American Idol*. It makes grown men cry and helps their daughters to sleep peacefully at night.

Aleeka Kay Edwards *is a twenty-three-year-old Guyanese immigrant who grew up in Queens, New York. She discovered her interest in visual production during her year at NBC in Burbank, California. She graduated from Brown University and now does script coverage for New Amsterdam Entertainment in Manhattan.*

I will complete my passages
Learn a new nature
Become a part of those sweet stories foretold
And with much departure from ignorant love
I will love myself and protect my soul
Treating myself as though God was me
Evolution—completely.
—Kimberly Y. Peters, "Crash Test Dummy"

My Nana Taught Me

by Suheir Hammad

My nana taught me
Speak up for me cause
Even my mama don't know
What it's like to live here where
And how I live only I know

My nana told me folks
Didn't listen to young black women
(never girls) when she was one
So I better talk as loud as I can about what
I want

I want
To be free where I live and to choose
How I live

I mean, do I have to have the answers just to get my rights?

Do I have to play ball or box to be seen
Do I have to shake my ass to get attention
Do I always have to act out
On the subway
In the classroom

In the street
Just so someone can hear me

My nana taught me
By never looking low
Head always high
(even when they sent their dogs after her)
Always carried herself like a lady
(ladies just rich and white and that's all made up anyway)

But even what's made up seems impossible to expose alone

What did your nana teach you?

Suheir Hammad *is a thirty-two-year-old Palestinian-American poet born in Jordan and raised in Brooklyn.*

Smurf Hunting

by Dondrie Burnham

Back before I knew
    what it was that men wanted
    the dirty treasure that starts wars that ravage women and
      murder me
Back when a smile was just a smile
    a nod was just a nod
    and god bless you was reserved for sneezing and Sundays
Back before I knew
    that I should be afraid
    that I should dance a jig and put on a show
    Be seen not heard and never let my feelings go
Back before I knew
    what fuck was
    when innocence lingered like cheap cologne
    and naïveté draped me like a shroud
    when I could graze the fields and soak in sunshine
I welcomed
    the hunter, the predator, the wolf in sheep's clothing
    my man, my idol: cleverly disguised as a daddy/lover all in one
and just as I began to relish my security blanket
    my safety net
    fire met passion
      passion met desire

and love crept like a coward out the back door
slowly but surely my cavern began to cave
> the walls became too narrow and the ceiling collapsed
> the bottom fell out
but my soul clung to this dwelling
> this hideout
> this place that I had long ago outgrown
because by now I was paralyzed by fear
and I had come to idolize you
> to hold you up like a golden god
> Adonis meet Zeus
> meet my God my King
as part of my idolatry I had began to study
> to watch and observe my place
> my position
> as woman
> as black woman
> deserted on this island of love
and terror replaced fear
and horror replaced terror
> my heart and soul flooded
> floating like driftwood in a sea of loneliness
> safety snatched
> protection plundered
> love lost
because by now I had discovered the danger of my treasure
> how skillfully it was hunted
> how easily it had been taken
> and how there would always be a hunter
> > a predator
> > looking to pillage the spoils
so my soul became restless
> waking from hibernation
> shouting indignations and incantations
> unleashing skeletons

shell-shocked by the sheer absurdity of life
     of love
and if I built a wall around myself
     a world around myself and I never let you penetrate
          never let your sun stream through my valley
Would I remain . . the hunted?
Because back before I knew what fuck was
     I knew what love was
but love crept like a coward out the door

Dondrie Burnham *is a twenty-five-year-old African-American actress and poet originally from Tennessee and currently residing in Harlem. Every thirty seconds a woman's heart is shattered, and she wrote this in the wake of one such quake.*

I am a woman because I throw rocks at your window at 3 a.m. Wake the fuck up!
—Girlstory, "Mamita"

kisses in tupperware

by Fly Yvonne O. Etaghene

your body is a familiar path I've walked a thousand times to my favorite place.

it's february
and I am kissing you for may today, kissing you for next tuesday, for next month, for a few hours from now when you are sleeping in mount vernon, miles away from me in harlem. I put your kisses in tupperware to be devoured later in a hungry moment. you asked me why I was kissing you like I was never going to see you again; you told me for a long time, I am all you have known and wanted. I started crying.

I think people see you as calm and reserved but I know you love, know your love as full of fire and heat. I know your passion, *I know you*, when your tongue is diving into me, your hands tight around my waist, your body arching into mine, your moans loud, your lips a dark pink, your teeth biting into me, I know you there, like that, full of heat, spilling onto my body, your fingers fast, your words pouring into my ear painting wet, lustful choreography our bodies dance out on this bed. *I know you like that.*

what is this they say about letting go? *let go?*
I am the hold-on queen, the clutter princess, the gonna-keep-this-just-in-case-I-need-it-someday lady. I keep things closer than people; I

have walked away from many women but you I want to keep ever so
close to me.
neither one of us wants to let go of us,
we hold on when it hurts, take breaths, step back, come back, make
love, cook, touch, laugh, scream.
you and I—
how many poems have been born between us?
in agony, desire and bliss? our lips
have uttered many pretty, ugly things—some of the pretty
and many of the ugly things were mine, I admit.
my love,
you are my family,
I have cried before you tears no one else has seen and tonight
my fingers sketch these words searching for meaning, *I will not let
you go,* I pray for the strength to trust that I do not have to hold onto
us so tightly, I pray for the clarity to trust we will still be *love,*
my love
even if we are not lovers.

Fly Yvonne O. Etaghene *is a twenty-five-year-old Nigerian woman-loving-woman poet raised in Ithaca, New York.*

I love you but I don't like you
I want you but I don't need you
and furthermore,
I think you're a coward.
—Dondrie Burnham, "Yellow Belly"

My Relationship with Me

by Deanna Kubota

Just a poem for myself. Not for some ex-boyfriend or some
    parent long
disowned. Just for me.
Just D. Not Deanna Kweana Kubota, not Ms. Kubota, and
    certainly not
"baby." I don't give into sexist stereotypes.
Just a poem about D. The writer, the singer, the lover, the crazed
    child who
beats her clammy fists on reality hoping it will break.
The punk-attic-metal-head-don't-wanna-be-what-you-want-for-me-
    just-want
to-be-me girl. The pretty, cute, sexy, flirtatious, tenacious D. The
    lyrical mad
scientist cackling about rhyme schemes and words that just don't
    rhyme at
all, like orange.
The musician, pianist/trumpet player and everything she can
    grabber.
Just a page or two about a girl, a chick, a tomboy mamma's-daddy's
    girl,
freak on a leash, a two-year-old in a sixteen-year-old's body with a
    ninety-nine-year-old
mind.

Just a rant about D. A cant about D. A long never-ending story
    about D.
Because she always talked about others and for once she can tell
    them who,
what, when, where, and why D.
I'll tell you why D.
Because she is me.

Deanna Kubota, *eighteen, is an angst-riddled Japanese and Yugoslavian
teen who lives on Maui.*

I've come to the understanding that I don't
want to set myself up for a lifetime of sadness and heartache. You're obviously not
happy with yourself, so how could you be what
I need? I'm starting to feel criticism, judg-
ment, fear, hostility, resentment, anger,
frustration, all these ugly feelings I've worked
to release over the years. I love you so much,
but you aren't healthy for me.
—Christina Massey, "Tortured Soul"

His thoughts are like a wide net of sunlight on a unkempt lake,
Or a disco light on speed for a single
dancer's sake . . .
And one has to change rhythm if she
wants to make a life with him.
—Annie Bacon, "The Battle Cry of Poetic Polygamy"

R-E-S-P-E-C-T

by Shannon McLaughlin

When I was little, just before my parents decided to get their first divorce, this is how it played out: "Blah blah blah, blah blah." BLAH, BLAH, blah blah." BLAH BLAH BLAH." "BLAH—BLAH!"

This would inevitably conclude with the slam of the front door, a tire kicking up pebbles in the driveway, and sniffles from my mom in the living room. Our house was small. My sister and I heard a lot.

Marriage, then, seemed a roller coaster of love and disdain, laughter and silence. Very polar.

And so I grew from a disappointed-in-her-parents young girl into a worldly, cynical, not-too-trusting young woman, who thought it very chic to hold the institution of marriage in contempt. My view on marriage, then, as echoed by Ambrose Bierce:

"Bride: A woman with a fine prospect of happiness behind her."

Now, as often happens with young women, my view of the world has shifted slightly as I have morphed into the wise, strong woman I am meant to be. Equipped with this wisdom, and a very fine man, I have opened my mind and heart to other ideas, and marriage now holds new meaning for me. And as I look at that ring upon my finger, I am awed, once again, at just how good sharing your life with another can be.

Marriage, for me, includes love, support, care, laughter, insight, and neck kisses that shoot bolts of lightening right through to the tips of my toes.

Yes, I did it. I got married, and you know what? I am happier in this relationship than I have ever been. But what, you ask, is the difference between living together without the ring, without the little certificate that says you are bound to this other person? I did that, too, shacked up with this man I married, for four lovely years, before exchanging those bands.

I don't know what changes occur when you say "I do." I have no idea. But there is something tangible, palpable, when you look into his or her eyes and say two short words. Commitment, for me, has brought a peace that I didn't possess in our simple cohabitation. Everything that was mine before is ours, for good and for bad. But the laughs are shared now, too, and the beauty of an autumn day. Someone marks the special occasions with me, and someone holds me when my heart feels broken down by the wearying confusion of the world outside.

A phrase I now find utterly distasteful as a married woman: "Marriage is a lot of work." You hear that a lot when you are engaged, often delivered with a knowing nod of the head. You know what I think? I think that phrase provides a crutch for the poor souls who married the wrong person. Yes, marriage can be challenging. Sharing your physical and mental space with another requires some compromise. Sure, we got issues, sometimes we even argue, but no one walks out of that door over a disagreement. We work it out, communicate, and respect each other as individuals.

And that is it. Respect. No secrets, no self-help books, no pharmaceutical intervention. When I was thirteen, I read a Confucius saying about a reed bending in the wind. I can't say that it has served as a guiding principle in my life, and I can dig in my heels quite well, thank you, but being the reed sometimes doesn't hurt, and sometimes it feels good to be the wind, too. My marriage is my home, and when I think about it, even really hard, I wouldn't change a thing.

Shannon McLaughlin, paying homage to the Queen of Soul, is from Denver, Colorado.

The Dreaded D Word

by Marti M. Champion

You want a what?! I never knew how powerful one word could be—a word that never crossed my mind when I made a commitment to you. I guess I misunderstood what you meant when you said, "I do." Those two words obviously did not touch you the way they touched me. "I do" meant you were my partner in life. "I do" meant you would have faith in us. "I do" meant you were committed to me. I thought this was supposed to be "'til death do us part." But if I think about it, I, as your wife, died the day you uttered one word. Divorce.

Almost sixteen years—wow. I have no idea what is to become of this relationship. In addition to losing my best friend, I am losing the dreams I had for the two of us. At thirty-four, I never thought I would have to go back to dreams of my own by myself.

Please forgive me. I gave up who I was in order to become who you wanted me to be. I tried to change who I was at my core. I let both of us down in my effort to become something or someone who was worthy of being your wife. In the end, I probably shouldn't have tried so hard—maybe I wasn't meant to be your wife. And guess what—I am OK with that now.

Marti M. Champion is a recovering romantic who is trying to give up her rose-tinted glasses.

You Can Be Right, or You Can Be Happy

by Ghana-Imani

What the fuck are *you* choosing? Do you really want to bitch about the socks on the floor *again?* Dishes were left in the sink, garbage not taken out; heartburn for that? Please!

Don't get me wrong, if you're going to partner up, you need a real *partner.* We're not their mothers, sisters, or bosses. We stand beside them, not behind them or in front of them—no matter who makes more money or who stays home with the kids. If it's a healthy relationship you seek partnership.

But just like in a business deal, partnerships have their deals, negotiations, *compromises.* Everybody's got to pull their weight to keep the company of Me and You, Baby, Incorporated up and running. So what was in your contract? Neatness, or compassion? Yes I know the hamper is *right there* and how much effort could it *possibly* take to just drop the fucking clothes in the hamper as opposed to on the floor. You're right! But . . .

Is he holding you when you cry about the promotion you didn't get? Rubbing your feet when you do double shifts? Telling you, showing you, how much he loves, appreciates, and respects you? Is he praying with you? Building with you? Talking about the future, saying always "we" and "us"? Or only "I" and "me"? Is he feeding your mind, body, and soul? Studying the you that was so he can please the woman that is and shall be?

And you want to fight about the socks. Again.

But there he is before you: a man of integrity, passions, humility, intelligence, purpose, and, oh, how he makes you laugh! How you wanna live this one out? Honey, you can be right . . . or you can be happy.

Choose your words carefully. Pick your battles thoughtfully. Love fiercely. No one is ever going to tout your victories over toilet seats and soiled laundry in your list of accomplishments when you're dead and gone. But they'll all remember that great love.

Ghana-Imani is a thirty-something poet, writer, performer, and diva living, laughing, and loving in Brooklyn, New York. She claims the entire African continent as her ancestral homeland, by way of North Carolina, Dominican Republic, and Haiti, which would explain her love of grits and porridge.

Ain't Gonna Be Nobody's Second Best

by Jennifer Poe

Ain't gonna be nobody's second best.
I go first.
Numero uno,
Numbre une.
Translated into get your stiff dick away from me.

I always regret the day I set foot in your home.

So many times my knees fell . . .
To the ground . . .
As my tears memorized every sound . . .
That communicated from your lips and fingertips,
Into my ears, in my e-mail.
I sing all your cruel words in my head like a sad love song.
Then I realize you're the one who did wrong.
Making me out to be manipulative and slutty.

You're the one with insanity.
Go ahead.
Point
Blame
Lie

Screw
Cheat
Cause I ain't nobody's second best.

Jennifer Poe is a twenty-year-old African-American filmmaker and poet living in New York City.

Ritual of Empowerment

Fierce Conversations

In Susan Scott's book, *Fierce Conversations,* she asserts that "wherever we are in our lives and most specifically in our relationships, we have arrived 'here' one conversation at a time." Scott defines a fierce conversation as one in which we come out from behind ourselves into the conversation and make it *real.*

Take a moment and think about the most important relationships in your life.

If you could rate the quality of your communication with each person on a scale of one to ten, how would you score?

What's your vision for the kinds of relationships you want to have?

Who are the kinds of people you want to be in relationship with?

What are the conversations you have been unable or unwilling to have that, if you were able to have them, might change everything?

When was the last time you had a fierce conversation?

Following this page is a Fierce Conversations Commitment Sheet. Without censoring yourself, list at least five people in your life with whom you are overdue for a fierce conversation, and what kind of conversation you need to have with them (about resolution of conflict, acknowledgement, opportunity, or support, and so on). Set yourself a deadline if you can. Scott says that while no single conversation is guaranteed to change anything, one single conversation can.

Fierce Conversations Commitment Sheet

Completion-Acknowledgement-Support-Opportunity

I, _____, in honor and celebration of my commitment to building healthy relationships, agree to have fierce conversations with the following five people by (insert date here):_____.

1.

2.

3.

4.

5.

We Got Stats!

➡ Studies show that nearly a **quarter of married women will cheat** during their marriage. If you include other forms of intimacy, such as emotional or sexual intimacy without actual intercourse, that figure rises by 15% to 20%. —Lonnae O'Neal Parker, *Essence* (2003)

➡ 7 in 100 of women married more than once have a husband 6 or more years younger than they are. —Wikipedia

➡ **Divorce is highest for women between the ages of 25 and 29.** —Shelly Amanstein. iVillage (2001)

➡ Of the more than 6,000 **same-sex marriages** conducted in the United States, **more than 2/3 have been female couples.** —Ken Maguire. *The Advocate* (2005)

➡ More than a quarter of working women, including mothers, spend at least some of their **nights and weekends at work.** —American Federation of Labor

➡ An Ohio University study showed that women whose mothers reported **cohabitation** were 57% more likely to cohabitate themselves. —United Press International

➡ As of 2000, **the most common household type in the U.S. is people living alone**: 27 million American households consist of a person living alone, compared to 25 million households with a husband, wife, and child.

—U.S. Census Bureau (2005)

➡ **Marital rape** accounts for 25% of all rapes, affecting more than 75,000 women each year.

—National Coalition Against Violence

➡ 41% of American women ages 15 to 44 have **lived with an unmarried different-sex partner** at some point in their lives. —Centers for Disease Control and Prevention (2002)

➡ **People who were unhappy about the 2000 elections were 8 times more likely to experience a rise in sexual activity.** —Becky Ebenkamp, *Brandweek* (2001)

Chapter 6

Holding the Planet
Motherhood, Mother US

I have four kids.
Amy, thirteen. Clara, ten. Louis, six. Lori, four.
My husband, George, is forty-three
But I dress him up, wipe his ass, and breastfeed him, too—
All with love.
—Lenelle Moïse, "Time" from the We Got Issues! Performance Piece

JLove Rants

I've enjoyed two great pregnancies, in love with the life growing within me and exquisitely happy. Both my deliveries, on the other hand, were earth-shattering. The word "pain" cannot even begin to describe what giving birth felt like to me.

With my first, I labored through a twenty-nine-hour natural birth. With my second, despite my "natural-only" friends, I had an epidural, and my labor, although long, was going fine. Until the beeping machines brought doctors running, and in less than three minutes my son had to be vacuumed out of my womb.

The sound of a silent newborn is the sound of fear.

The pain of my raw insides being "cleaned up" was not why I was screaming, as I watched six doctors rushing and surrounding my very still and very silent baby.

"What's wrong with my baby?" I yelled, but no one heard me. "Tell me what's happening!" My shrieks were just background noise to the doctors urgently discussing whether my son would live or die. I looked at the grave face of my husband on one side and my mother on the other.

"Apgar is only at three," a doctor said. "We've got to intubate, now!" I was lying on the bed, straining my neck to get a glimpse of what was happening; the doctors backs were blocking my view of my child. I knew what Apgar scores were—the vital signs determining the health of the baby. Perfect is ten, and normally healthy is seven.

My baby was three.

"I want my baby." My hysteria was climbing. Every time I spoke or tried to sit up, a gush of blood exited my womb. The doctor who was still between my legs urged me to calm down.

My breath was coming faster and faster. "It's my fault," I sobbed to my husband, "I shouldn't have induced labor—he wasn't ready."

Camilo was two weeks late. My OB-GYN assured me inducing had no risks, and my mother, whom I *had* to have by my side, had flown in from Denver. I couldn't imagine going through the process without her. So we decided to induce."

"It's not your fault," my husband said. I was shaking my head back and forth. He grabbed my arm. "Look at me, look me in the eyes!"

"No, no, no! Get me my child! I want to see my baby!"

My husband took hold of my head with both of his hands, and forced me to look at him.

"Focus, Jenny, focus! Camilo needs you right now! Stop crying, we need to pray!" he said forcefully, and then, more softly, weeping, "Our son needs us now."

We prayed, and we prayed, and we prayed.

There was still no sound from my son when they wheeled him out of my room into the neonatal intensive care unit.

It was ten hours before I knew that my son was going to survive.

Two weeks later, I sat on my couch with my baby Camilo. I felt the sweet tug and release while he breastfed, looking up into my eyes.

I have never experienced joy like that.

I lived in bliss the first year of Camilo's life. I was breastfeeding, doing some consultant jobs here and there, and taking care of my older son, Gabriel, who was school-age.

But the journey of motherhood is not static. It can change from blissful peace to chronic insanity at the drop of a dime. We can't talk about motherhood or parenthood fully without acknowledging the whole spectrum from that bliss to crazy obsessive worrying about things like whether vaccinations cause autism and how to protect your child from playground bullies, guns, and violent video games.

And then there are the bad days, the days when you snap and yell at your child for spilling juice for the fifteenth time, or give in to greasy-ass McDonald's and blaring cartoons because you're too tired to fight it.

What do you do when you feel you're just not good enough? When you can't wake up; get ready for work; get the kids dressed, fed, packed up, and dropped off at day care and school (on time with no tears); walk into the office by 9:00 a.m., work work work until 5:15 p.m.; run out the door; pick up child number one, pick up child number two; traffic traffic traffic (outside); "I'm hungry, I have to go to the bathroom, he hit me" (inside). Home. Park. Unload.

Yes, we *finally* made it in the house. Now, if you could just make it through dinner, homework, brushing teeth, and bedtime story, your day will be over. Just to start it again tomorrow.

Motherhood is a choice. A series of choices, actually.
It requires patience, persistence, and perseverance
Dialogue, dedication and decisions
A third eye, and always an extra set of hands.

It requires a sense of humor
Money and resources (don't believe the hype that love is all you need—your child needs health insurance and so do you)

Foresight, insight, and hindsight
Passion and compassion
Energy, boundless . . .

And love. But everything above equals love. And it is more than that.

It is waking up, everyday, and pledging to be the best mother you can be. And knowing that it is worth it. Your baby is worth it. You are worth it.

In those divine moments when you're holding your kids, and they're looking at you as if you are the queen of the world, when they kiss you with sticky lips and say "wuv you, Mommy," you know that there is nothing more important, more precious, more rewarding than this.

Welcome to motherhood.

Bold

Asia One

Asia's initial embarkment into Hip-Hop was in Denver, Colorado (her hometown), where she opened Denver's first Hip-Hop shop and workspace called "La Casa del Fonk." The founder of the B-Boy Summit and No Easy Props, Asia gives workshops across the country, produces Hip-Hop dance DVDs, and performs with No Easy Props Crew and the Essential Rockers. She lives with her four-year-old daughter, Yasmin Joy.

Age:
35
Cultural Identity:
Chinese Hip-Hop American
Born In:
Denver, Colorado
Education:
College
Occupation:
B-girl Icon
Economic Class:
High to mid to low
and back again
Marital Status:
Single but involved
Registered to vote:
Yes

❶ What has been one of the greatest moments of being a mother?

For a long time I wanted a soul mate, someone who would have unconditional love for me, who would be a constant, permanent part of my life. I thought the want was for a man, but once I was pregnant I knew it was for the life in me, my daughter, Yas. And she is truly that, like a lil' doll, *la maniquita*. She never gives me a hard time, a true angel. We struggled together, but were taught valuable lessons in life about the yin and yang, the natural flow of things.

We have each other for life and our spirits are bound forever. I still don't think we deserve her, and I remind her pops of that often. I won't see her suffer. Her destiny here on earth is to thrive and succeed far beyond my heights.

❷ What has been one of the worst moments for you as a mother?

It pains me to think that most of my irrational/bad parent moments happened during a time when I was in an extremely abusive relationship, involving a bunch of people. Her pops was literally MIA in Miami. I wish I had been, too, since the hell that I was in was too much to cope with, much less to raise a child in. I will say that I think I really held it down by her in all periods, but I was not living consciously, or following my conscience either. How can a Vegan consume Hennessey? That sauce will kill you. I was drinking and picked up the bad habit of smoking blunts. Great. I was self-medicating to deal with my pain and frustration; I could see it but couldn't do anything about it.

❸ How do you create balance, between your needs and the needs of your child, family, and so on?

We have to interact together harmoniously so I put aside other desires—like having a super career—that do not necessitate my full attention. We are as One, and as long as our spiritual side is correct we will be in balance. It is always when I am feeling unbalanced that bad times occur. Yogis believe that every woman must meditate, sweat, love, and of course do Yoga daily. We women are emotional beings in flux with the moon. Thus, we must learn to love ourselves as emotional beings, ruled by our intuition, and accept that we function from different areas than men do. It's the polarity of this ebb and flux that allows us to come together to create life. I also understand our need to be away from each other and the growth that occurs because of our separation. If you can learn to let go, it will always come back!

❹ What is the greatest personal change you have had to undergo since becoming a mother?

Our Id is so strong that we can lead a really selfish existence of me, me, me. A mom-to-be has the crazy realization that this big fat prego state of being is the last time she will ever be alone again with just her life to deal with. Wow! When we were rollin', we were out all day every day! Drugs, lawless behavior. I think I have been an outlaw since birth really. My daughter came to let me know my mission was to be a mom, to procreate, to continue the seed, to have a sidekick!

A good mother is so many things, like a gift unfolding daily. I remember a time not too long ago when I didn't get along with my mom, and we had no real relationship. I think it was mutual; we just let things drift, neither one really caring. I wasn't living right—now I see the light! My shift of consciousness and the birth of my daughter brought us back together! A good mom spends time with her kids, is always there for them. I would never leave my child with anyone I didn't fully trust with her life.

❺ How does one's economic reality affect child-rearing?

I see the kids from the ghetto hoods and always am touched by their spirit. They create their own culture; when multiculturalism wasn't that hip, they created Hip-Hop. You know what families I look up to? Mexican families and Filipino families for being big, close knit, and happy. In Mexican neighborhoods, where I spent many years, your house will not get robbed, nor will you have any drama, unless you're trying to move weight there.

My daughter was born when I lived in this old-school toonerville gang 'hood. I lived across the street from one of the oldest families in that 'hood, who were there for over two hundred years. Anyhow it was a little barrio, but I keep it cool over there, no drama. My daughter Yasmin was born, we call her Ya Ya or Yas. She immediately wanted to hang out like everyone else, run around, drink twenty-five sodas, and eat hot Cheetos. Both of these things together are like a toxic chemical. It made it hard at times to keep her away from that and still keep her happy. Yas knows ultimately that I know what is best for her and will keep her healthy and safe. It is safe to say that the environment you live in is a direct factor in your kid's life. I am glad I don't have so much as to spoil Yas to the point of her not understanding that you don't get everything you want, u get what u get! This is the creed in our house. Our children learn to empathize at a young age with poverty and with those who don't have "nothing." At the same time, you want to give your kids what you didn't have. We scoff at the rich and feel sorry for the poor, feeling guilty at times for success with money.

My lovely ones out there, you may be mothers one day sooner than you think. It is our purpose, our animalistic nature and spirit. There is no right or wrong time; that spirit that will be your child has chosen her/his physical form at this moment in time to teach you one of the most valuable lessons that you will ever learn. Understand, warrior women, that at the moment you decide you are going to be a mom, you must make the commitment to raise the child by yourself if need be. You are that child's sole supporter, the end of the food chain. *If* you can accept this, you can be a mom, cuz the man may separate from you and go on about his own life forgetting his responsibility to the life that needs him. I am with you. We as Wombed Beings, moms, are in tune with each other to help support and guide each other. Hello!—that is why people with kids hang out.

In Life we go . . .

Disney Freak

by Caridad De La Luz

I was wondering, are you a Disney Freak?

That disturbs me because I am a mother, and most of Disney's characters don't even have a mother. Most of those stories start out with the mother dying or just being mysteriously absent from the family. If there *is* a mother, she is usually an evil *step*mother who abuses or tries to kill the kid. Walt Disney must have hated women. Disney's mother was probably so abusive that it had him talking to mice, angry ducks, and dumb dogs. Crazy, right? But check it: Cinderella's mother? Dead. Snow White's mother? Dead. Bambi's mother? Shot. Now, Belle and Jasmine were raised by their dads, but without one nice thing to say about their mothers. The only one that I remember who had a good mother was Dumbo, but then look at the name Disney gave him. That's messed up, right?

Let's examine *Beauty and the Beast,* shall we? There was a good mother figure in that: Chip's mom, Mrs. Potts. Her life was working in the kitchen, serving tea all damned day. She was nice and brave enough to speak up about the Beast's temper when he was verbally abusing Belle and had even knocked her around a couple of times. But Belle forgave him; after all, he did save her from the wolves and gave her a bunch of books to read. Progressive. Meanwhile, Lumiere was sexually harassing the staff and Gaston was telling his three bitches that it was still all good whether he married Belle or not.

Is this teaching children that male chauvinism, infidelity, and domestic violence are OK? That a woman's voice should not be heard and that nobody needs a mother? Come on, Disney didn't even give Pinocchio a mother—not even a wooden mother. The only good mother figure was a fairy, as if good mothers don't exist in the real world. OK, I know, Pinocchio wasn't a real boy, so he didn't need to have a mother, 'cause a trespassing cricket and an idiot savant wood-carver would be just as good, if not better, than having a real mother.

It's sad, so *motherf*king* sad.

Caridad De La Luz, *aka LA BRUJA, is a twenty-seven-year-old Puerto Rican poet, activist, Hip-Hop–reggaeton artist, and mother from New York City.*

I know mad Hip-Hop mamis and papis raising their kids up in the culture; we need more of this, though. No more asking, "Is it cool to bring my kids?" Of course it is cool, it should be! —Asia One, B-girl

Mami, I can see your dried nipples, wet only by my frustrating tears as I pulled at the skin of your breasts, tasting nothing.
—Gabriela Erandi Rico, "My Mother Is My Story"

The New Math

by Karima Grant

Once
upon a time
when knowledge and wisdom brought forth the understanding that
      we were all
Gods and Earths
and We held the power
to organize
build or destroy
this Babylon
We set out to work to the pulse of justice.
Late fall,
the world bursting into flame,
Calling,
me responding weakly,
on my knees moaning,
breathing,
pushing,
praying,
Your eyes held me still.
Me
who had fought the police/fought the men/fought the world
(fought myself)
felt the bittersweet chilliness of real fear

What if I fail?
Make the road by walking, the ancestors whispered.
Women who strap babies onto hips, bellies, backs
continue the work.
Have no other bearing.
And so in a world of compromise and contradiction
I tuck homemade cookies into snack boxes
While the picture of me
all those lifetimes ago
grows dusty above my desk.
Looking at pictures now
of me back then
you and your brothers struggle to find the resemblance
"that *you*, mommy?" you giggle.

Looked up one day and you were seven.
Eyes fastened to me still.
    What do you see?
The war still rages brutal
for the hearts, minds, souls, and bodies of our most beloved.
Yet my weapons of defense,
pen, pad
get harder to reach
through the elaborate maze
of little needs and wants,
boo-boos and imagined hurts,
old souls leaning into mama warmth.

Seven,
we ordained,
was the number of God.
Running in breathless,
snatching me away from my tap, tap, typing.
I am Writing.
Sanctified moment.

But there you stand anyway,
chest heaving,
hair standing,
untamed,
Brilliant halo.
"Did you see me, did you see me?"
The desk is positioned by the window
and yes,
I watched,
equally breathless as you flew,
no training wheels,
pumping hard,
no training wheels
head thrown back in the quiet majesty of your own single, solitary
    power.
(Looked up and you were seven.)
"Did you see *me?*" you insist.
I am writing this because my heart threatens to break.
Open wide.
Make space for the utter newness of who yet I have to be,
of who you will make me,
of who I have become.
"Did you see me?" you demand.
And the yes cushioned near my heart
will make me bigger than I have ever been,
stronger than I will ever know.
Yes, my sweet,
I see you clear.

*Writer, teacher, and administrator **Karima Grant** is a thirty-four-year-old mother of three. Author of adult and children's fiction and nonfiction, she currently lives in Dakar, Senegal.*

Remnants of Isabella

by Ashlyn N. Shockley

I knew Isabella had arrived
    when I was ten days late
Damn girl didn't even RSVP
Didn't give me time to bring out the welcome mat
All pretty and pink with little roses
    Saying "do not disturb"
    My life.
But she came
    Just like he had
    inside
My mind was a whirlwind of nausea
    And Bible verses
And already she was bringing the pain:
Damn, love ain't supposed to hurt this much

My conscience caught glimpses
    Of ash-brown pigtails
    And sea-green eyes like her Daddy's
    Every bit as tiny and feisty as her Mommy

She would laugh
And whine
    And finally fall asleep in my arms sucking on her thumb
And rubbing her left ear

Blew kisses to strangers, made wishes in penny fountains,
    Daddy's girl,
Mommy's little monster

And on her sixth birthday
    Daddy taught her to ride
I wished she would ride away
    Past split-levels
        Those damn white picket fences
Disapproving suburbia
    Southern Baptist Sunday School
And leave me to my misery

There were plenty of skinned knees and boo-boos after that

Dreamed of cotton-candy-pink prom dresses
    Sweet sixteens, first dates
And spring
    Her birthday was in April

She would laugh
    And cry
And fall asleep in my arms

I didn't want her
    To want for anything

I didn't want her
    Thought it better I burn in Hell alone

Figured it was better I bear the burden alone
    Than pass it off to someone so unassuming
Maybe hide out in church
    Isn't that where the sinners congregate?

Wasn't ready for bear hugs and Huggies, "M o m m y!"
   Or the pitter-patter of little feet
      Leaving scars all over my heart

So I promptly deposited ash-brown tendrils
    and the innocence of sea-green eyes into a cannula

Childhood was worth
    Exactly four
       hundred
and
ten dollars

Daddy put it on credit

Left her soul dang
        l
         i
           n
             g in purgatory
and caught the next flight to nowhere

Ashlyn N. Shockley is a twenty-two-year-old African-American crisis counselor with the National Abortion Federation, where she has counseled hundreds of women. As an expectant mother, she understands the need for improvements within the health care social welfare systems and has strived to do her part. She currently lives in Virginia.

To Whom It May Concern

by E. Anne Zarnowiecki

Sitting down, I focus my thoughts so that I can express my rage eloquently. I mentally delete expletives and replace them with a formal register. The people at the Patient Relations Department of Children's Hospital will be more likely to digest my letter if I keep it businesslike, I reason. Having reworded my diatribe a million times in the shower, car, and grocery store, I feel a sense of readiness. I am tired of rolling over and playing possum.

I try and find the exact words for the letter because I want it to be clear that the way we were treated in the hospital was unacceptable and demeaning. I am queer and living in the Midwest, I remind myself. I'm accustomed to making bland statements more palatable for my listener. But now everything is different. Now I have a son to think about—a son whose biological connection to me seems always to be in question. My relationship to him, my love for him, is scrutinized not only by the doctors and nurses who paraded through our hospital room, but also by everyone we meet during our daily activities.

I think of our run-in with the hospital social worker. She scanned the room when she first walked in with her tailored suit and clipboard. Looking me up and down, it was obvious that she felt something just wasn't quite right. I answered questions gently, so as not to offend any straight white sensibilities. She shifted uneasily in her seat as I explained for the seven-thousandth time how the accident happened. She stopped me, midstory, to ask if I am the babysitter or roommate. My teeth ground in frustration as I reminded her that I am Javier's other mom. My politically correct terms went over her head, so how do I make it click that the woman sitting next to me is my wife and that this little boy is my son? Would she still have been convinced that I was abusing my child if we were a heterosexual couple? Maybe we would be sitting together chuckling about how dads can be careless and how children fall so quickly. But instead, her face registered disbelief while I recounted the accident. We sat in tense silence as she wrote notes for her report. Her pen scratched furiously and accusatorily. I could practically hear her say a little mental prayer for the soul of this baby being raised in sin. I sat, taking deep breaths, trying to talk myself out of breaking the clipboard and shredding her papers. The anger rising inside of me was looking feverishly for a venue. But I knew everything that was at stake so I slapped a smile on my face; I became polite and unassuming. This woman had the power to tear my family apart.

As I contemplate my letter of formal complaint to the hospital, I think of the other ways in which our gay interracial family encounters homophobia. Though I have been there since the moment of my son's conception, I have no legal rights to him in the state of Ohio. If something were to happen to my partner, her parents would have more legal standing for custody than I would. If he needs medical care, I am forced to wait for my wife to come and sign the papers. We can't file our taxes jointly, nor are we all on the same insurance plan. If upcoming legislation is passed, gay people will be banned from adopting or foster parenting in the state of Ohio. Instead of worrying about buying safe, educational toys and saving for a college fund, I fight over custody rights and recognition of power of attorney.

I am determined to honor my beautiful little baby by confronting discrimination head-on. He will be aware from an early age that life is not always fair and that people don't always play nice. He will however, see his parents tackle bigotry as it comes. It is for him that I do not allow doctors or social workers to marginalize us. As I begin to write, I feel my anger transform to resolution.

To Whom It May Concern,

I am writing to register a formal complaint about the treatment my family received at Children's Hospital . . .

E. Anne Zarnowiecki is a twenty-eight-year old Cincinnati-living Caucasian lesbian. She loves working with Spanish bilingual students with disabilities. Anne has found that being with a black woman and having a biracial son who has a Latino name confuses the good folks of Ohio. She is dedicated to confronting bigotry and hatred.

Some days I am good at keeping things together; other days we lie in bed together, watch cartoons, and eat ice cream and popcorn all day and night. I'm corny, so often we play some Whitney, "I'm every woman, it's all in me!" and we dance around the living room with our deaf kitty.

—Rachel Raimist, filmmmaker

Silent Fertility

by Marla Teyolia

Silence falls on 16th Street and Park Avenue East
Between depression and alternative medicine
Two women stand
Reaching for the shelf next to the empty space that holds the second
    of three:
A Couple's Guide to In-Vitro Fertilization

We share a moment of silence
No words can capture this journey

I want to reach out to her, to touch her
To ask her a million questions:
How far along is she in this journey?
Who is her doctor?
How is she feeling?
Does *she* know what foods to eat that aid in implantation?

But instead, I am met with *silence*
With *shame*
With *compassion*
And *respect*

So I look away
Giving her the anonymity

To read this book alone
Free from the fear that someone, anyone
Might find out her secret

That she is
Infertile
Barren
Childless
Longing

Is that what defines us?
The power we hold between our legs?
Who do we become when we feel our body has betrayed us?
That your birthright is not mine

For years, those closest to me never knew my truth
The secret I kept hidden
Even from myself

The holistic warrior in me wants to believe that
If I take
This herb
Or
That tonic
Or
These clay poultices
That fresh-squeezed juice
That
I will be OK

The spiritualist in me wants to believe that
If I say
Just the right prayer
Or
Make the perfect offering to Ochun or Yemaya

That if I say
Nine rosaries
Or
Take flowers to the Virgin
That
It will be OK

But what happens to a woman
A woman of color
A voluptuous
Hourglass woman
With
Big
Beautiful
Childbearing
Hips

What happens when
The tonics
The prayers,
The dreams
The flowers
Don't work?

When your knees are sore from kneeling at the altar
When you start to become the woman you never thought you'd be
The one
Whose womb *cries out*
At every baby shower
At every friend who announces she's pregnant one more time
When all you want to do is cry out
"Why me?"

You find your strength then
After the tears

The heartache
The pain
The betrayal
You discover what you are made of
What you are capable of doing

For that one moment in time when you can tell your husband
"You're gonna be a dad"
There will be no words for that
And
The silence
Will
Be
Golden

Marla Teyolia, *actor, writer, all-around diva, loves life, laughter, making dinner with her husband, chilling with her girls, walking her dogs, and just being in the presence of the ocean.*

A good mother is a mom committed to learning how to parent. No one knows how to be the perfect parent. I am a good mom 'cause I listen, love, laugh, and teach. I am her rock, someone who she knows that she can turn to regardless.
—Lateefah Simon

What I Want For Her

by Millicent Walsh

I want for her to have more money than me, money to make her comfortable, be able to pay the bills on time, travel if she wants. But I want her to understand that money doesn't make you happy. We make our days our own; we create our reality as much as it creates us.

I want for her to be an independent girl, a strong woman, and each day I hope and pray that my example doesn't fail her, that my strength comes through more than my frustrations and that she draws from a well that doesn't run dry, because some days, man, I feel beaten down.

I feel beaten down by health challenges—I'm too young for rheumatoid arthritis! I'm too young to be slowed down, to have this pain in my joints. I don't want for her to have this kind of pain. I want for her to be healthy and strong and vital. I want for her to move, to feel her body work for her. I want for her to jump and run and play without fear that one day it just might not work at all, that one day she may have stacks of medical bills to pay instead of exciting travels to make. I want for her to forget about when that happened to me and so I try and forget.

I've got some pills now. They make me mostly better. Every day I move my body and rejoice in the simple pleasure of being able to. Sometimes I can't, but I still try everyday because I don't want her to be a person who gives up when things get tough. She sees me doing, striving, and she knows it's not always easy. I hope it teaches her that sometimes life is hard, but you can do it. You don't always have control over what happens, you may stumble, but you pick yourself up and you move.

And I hope she sees me smile through it just as much as she sees me grimace. I don't want her to worry; I don't want her to be afraid. But I want her to be real. There are good things and bad things in life.

I want for her to love herself as she grows and as her body changes, to embrace the curves that proclaim to the world that she is a woman. I want to have a party to celebrate her puberty, so she can hold her head high and hear stories from me and my women friends about our experiences. I want to usher that in with celebration because it is a blessing—and a curse. The blessing is that she may one day have a baby of her own; that she holds the power to give birth, to carry a child in her body and bring it forth, to begin her own journey of motherhood.

It's transformative, that journey. It changed me from who I was to who I am. I will always be a mother now. She is mine and I am hers for always. It's more amazing as she grows toward adulthood. I am so proud of my girl. I want for her to be proud of herself, to believe in herself, that she can do anything she wants to do. I want to give her that. As I take my own journey I teeter between believing in fate and believing in accountability, because some parts of my life are disappointing. I think it's important to believe. I write that on chalkboards at home, on the welcome screen for my cell phone. It's a good message for her; she still believes in magic in the world.

She is smart and adaptive. She is beautiful and funny. She is as much my teacher as I am hers and I am amazed at the grace with which she navigates all of her challenges. I want to be able to do the same for her.

Millicent Walsh, *lives in Denver, Colorado. She is a single mother to daughter Natasha Grace, and keeper of the dog, Boris, and the cat, Stella. She is currently browsing for lovers.*

Thoughts on the Road

by Allison Joy

Mother Nature's tears
Splash against and slip down
The windshield
Of my little red rented Neon,
And I aimlessly flip on
The wipers
That brush aside her sorrow
So brutally with indifference
That she weeps all the more.

I drive across her torso,
The weight of me and the car
Pressed into her side,
Traveling pathways we have carved
Into her flesh
That stretch out to the horizon
Who mourns the loss of her lush green kisses.

We roll over murals of roadway
Whose black tar and yellow paint
Butcher her beauty,
Blue skies choke
In tapestries of sunsets

Struggling to survive the onslaught,
Smothered in our exhaust,
Rolling hills leveled and buried.
Her screams go unnoticed,
The constant rumbling of big rigs too overbearing.

We have become anesthetized
From this destruction.
We see only efficiency.
We see only the fastest way
From point A to point B
Is to break ground,
Break her.
We gotta
Make that money,
Take that money,
We gotta bulldoze and chop down and cement over.
Over and over and over.
We gotta clear the way for our precious cargo—
Material capitalism packed away,
Prepped for shelves,
Poised to be stocked and consumed.

How easily we consume.
How easily we presume
It is all ours for the taking.
Breaking soul ties we once had
With her,
Littering her body
With our filth and abuses.

Mother who loved us so much
She offered all she had.
Cradled in her bosom
We have tasted her sweetness,

And she is now sore from our greed.
We take more
Than the both of us can afford.

I hear her cries now,
Our weary and broken Mother.
I see what we have done to her.
I focus on the rain,
Touch my fingertips to the glass
To trace its journeys
And I whisper,
"I am so sorry."

Allison Joy *is currently a performer in the We Got Issues! National tour, and makes damn good spicy brownies. This queer Filipina American believes in the strength of her sisters, community building, art as activism, grassroots organizing, loving honestly, linking arms with all oppressed peoples, and manifesting visions of liberation.*

My little boys, with sponges for brains, are learning a great deal about how to function in the world—they are learning this by watching me.
—Erin Sampson, *Motherhood and Feminism: The Stay-at-Home Struggle*

Ritual of Empowerment

Reclaiming Yourself and Reclaiming Your Sanity: Mommy's Time Out

When you feel like you've lost yourself in the role of mother, when you crave a night out without the responsibility of being in charge of another human being's life (and without the extra luggage of the baby bag, stroller, and age-appropriate snacks), it's time, ladies, to reclaim a little piece of yourselves. Tell everyone that you have two doctor's appointments in one day, thus giving you the whole afternoon off. (You can choose what the appointment is for, but mammograms always work.) You must treat this afternoon as Sacred non-mommy time. Here are some suggestions of what you can do:

- Get a massage
- Have a manicure and pedicure
- Go to a matinee movie, with a big bucket of popcorn, a soda, and candy (don't you love that salty-then-sweet thing?)
- Go shopping (but you can't buy for anyone but yourself)
- Get a haircut and color
- Go to the gym
- Take a leisurely walk in the park
- Take yourself to happy hour (two-for-one margaritas, anyone?)

Repeat this ritual at least monthly.

We Got Stats!

➡ **10 million women are single mothers.**
—U.S. Census Bureau (2001)

➡ In 2000, the **number of births among U.S. women ages 18 and 19** was 311,781. —Alan Guttmacher Institute

➡ 4 states—California, Illinois, Missouri, and Vermont—have implemented or encouraged the development of a **breastfeeding-awareness education campaign.** —National Conference of State Legislatures

➡ A study of family interactions spanning 3 generations and comparing the adult relationships of **children from single-mother households** with those from 2-parent households found that children who had warm, supportive relationships with their single mothers **formed satisfying, committed relationships with equal success** to those who had similar parent-child relationships in 2-parent homes. —Iowa State University (2001)

➡ **31 states**—California, Colorado, Connecticut, Delaware, Florida, Georgia, Hawaii, Illinois, Indiana, Iowa, Louisiana, Maine, Maryland, Minnesota, Missouri, Montana, Nevada, New Hampshire, New Jersey, New Mexico, New York, North Carolina, Oklahoma, Ohio, Oregon, Rhode Island, South Dakota, Utah, Texas, Vermont, and Virginia— **allow mothers to breastfeed in any public or private location.** —National Conference of State Legislatures

>

➤ **New York was the first state** in the nation to enact any form of **breastfeeding legislation** when, in 1984, the breastfeeding of infants was exempted from its criminal statute. In 1994, New York led the nation by amending its civil rights act to grant mothers an absolute **right to breastfeed in public.**

—Melissa R. Vance, La Leche League International

➤ **In 2002, there were more than 687,000 day care centers in the U.S.** —U.S. Census Bureau

➤ In 2003, there were 5.4 million **stay-at-home moms** in the U.S.; 39% were under the age of 35. —U.S. Census Bureau

➤ **If single working mothers earned as much as men in comparable jobs,** their family incomes would increase by nearly 17% and their poverty rates would be cut in half, from 25.3% to 12.6%. —American Federation of Labor

Chapter 7

Cease and Desist
The New Epidemic of Violence

JLove Rants

I was looking forward to going out that night; it had been a minute—and I definitely needed a break. My husband agreed to take the kids for the night. Digging through my closet, sipping on a Corona with old-school Tribe Called Quest serenading me, I find the skirt my girlfriend Lalania made for me, and the new shirt my sister lent me. I put on my outfit with accessories to match. As I'm applying my makeup, my girl-friend Wanda calls.

"Girl, I can't go. My babysitter fell through so I have to stay home—rain check?"

"Of course, I understand," I say.

But I'm upset. Wanda was going to drive, and I'm definitely planning on getting fucked-up. The twenty dollars I have in my cute red Brooklyn purse will pay to get in the club and have a couple of drinks, so I definitely don't have cab fare.

"Damn!"

I look at myself in the mirror and survey my outfit with a different lens.

Skirt: too short for the subway, will draw unnecessary attention.

Top: too low-cut. I could wear a scarf to cover up on the train. But then I'd have to carry it around the club all night.

Shoes: definitely can't wear no heels—can't run if I need to, not safe while walking in the dark down the five blocks to get to the L train.

Earrings: they're fake gold, but a junkie might just see the bling and go for it, seeking money for his next high.

Tribe Called Quest ends its serenade. My Corona has turned room-temperature and nasty. And I have nothing to wear.

I take off my makeup, put on my sweats, and climb into bed.

I'll never forget the day I bought my .45 Smith and Wesson. The bullets were actually harder to decide on than the gun. "Ma'am," explained the nice redneck gun salesman, "say you hafta use this here gun on an intruder in your home." He held up my gun for emphasis, talking to me like I was an idiot. "If you shoot this gun with regular bullets, they are gonna go right through your home walls and into the next apartment, and could then hit an innocent; it could hurt 'em pretty bad, maybe even kill 'em."

Well, I didn't want to *kill* anyone, which was my whole problem with the hollow-tip bullets: They ricochet throughout the entire body until stopped by an organ, making it more likely the victim will die.

I just wanted to be safe.

It was the first time I had ever lived alone. The only place I could afford on a nonprofit salary was near enough dope dealers and addicts that I felt unsafe, pure and simple.

What does it mean to live in a world that fundamentally does not allow women to live in peace? What does it mean to live in a world where women are seen as easy targets for the venting of fear, frustration, and madness?

Artist-activist Eve Ensler points out that when women are either raped, or living in fear of being raped, we have an epidemic on our hands. One look at the murder and sexual assault rates in this country and there is no doubt what she says is true. According to the U.S. Department of Justice's "Violence Against Women: A National Crime Victimization Survey Report":

- Every day, four women die in this country as a result of domestic violence.
- Even the most conservative estimates indicate two to four million women of all races and classes are battered each year.

- Every year, more than one million women are raped by their current or former male partners, some more than once.

But what about other crimes against women? We don't hear much about the rise in women-on-women crime, or the recent popularity of women in contact sports that breed violence, such as boxing and wrestling. The media doesn't cover the disproportionate increase in young women in our prison system, or the growing numbers of young women joining the military. Indeed, what was most disturbing to many people about the photos detailing the horrific torture at Abu Ghraib was the image of a young female soldier, Private Lynndie England, just twenty-three years old at the time, as one of the prime offenders of such inhumanity; how could this be?

The violence permeating our society has profound effects on all of us, as war continues to rage in all corners of the globe, as women continue to fall victim to the heavy hand of lovers and strangers, as women continue to perpetuate the cycle and take our own pain out on the most vulnerable of all, our children. Many teachers across the country lament the rate of self-imposed abuse and mutilation perpetrated by young girls who are so distraught about their lives and our world that they cut themselves in hopes of easing the pain, or, worse yet, commit suicide.

And yet, even amongst these dismal facts and statistics, we women rise!

Women who have experienced, perpetrated, or borne witness to violent acts are saying, here and now, *"No mas!* No more!" to violence in our communities, to violence against our sistas. Women are at the forefront in demanding an end to this senseless war. *No mas!* No more war!

Let *those* voices and images come to you, as you get ready for that well-deserved night out, as you walk down that dark street after your self-defense class, as you move through this world handling your business, rest assured.

We as a community of women have and will continue

To come together to heal, and end the

Violence.

P.S. With reservations, I bought the hollow tips. I still own the gun.

Bold

Chino Hardin

Chino Hardin, a youth organizer at the Prison Moratorium Project, joined PMP as an intern in the summer of 2001 and came onto PMPs full-time staff in February 2002. Chino brings personal experience with the New York City juvenile justice system to her organizing work. Her work has appeared in Off Our Backs, *the* Village Voice, Caribbean Life, *and numerous other community-based publications.*

Age:
25
Cultural Identity:
Black, Italian, and Indian
Born:
In Brooklyn, New York
Education:
Ninth grade
Occupation:
Organizer
Economic Class:
Poor
Marital Status:
Engaged
Registered to vote:
Yeah, I am

❶ How do you define violence?

Violence can be anything—a hit in the face, or the emotional abuse you receive during your whole life. It does not only play out on a physical plane but also on a mental level: This country passes down mental violence from generation to generation. For me, mental violence is the worst because if I get stabbed in the street, I could live through it—my body will mend—but the mental images and the memory of being stabbed is a mental, emotional, soul thing that is ever-continuing. Because I am scared I might carry a gun to protect myself, and then if I get into a conflict again, I might shoot somebody.

To me, violence is a breakdown of rational thought.

❷ How does violence uniquely affect you as a young woman?

I am surrounded and bombarded by it, even in the music I listen to. The mental stress plays out in so many ways, because when it builds up and I don't confront it, I have the possibility to physically explode toward somebody else and even toward myself.

I think I am a violent person—I am not violent to the point where I can't be rationalized with, but if you fuck with me or mines, I am going to hurt you. Violence is an everyday part of my life. I try not to internalize it and project it onto others. It's easiest to project it onto loved ones, because I know that they will give me that room; a stranger may retaliate and hurt me back. I am a logical person as well, so when I get angry or lash out, I try to check myself—if I say something fucked-up and my partner says it hurt her feelings, I look at what I did and I ask myself: Where did my reaction come from?

❸ What fuels your activism around violence?

I was in and out of jail from the ages of thirteen to twenty-one. The scariest thing about jail is that I got used to it. I learned how to navigate my way around. In jail, I was a predator—I would take advantage of the new girls, I would rob from people, I would beat up the other girls. It was only after I experienced someone I loved being raped while I was locked up that my heart softened. I used to mess with this one girl all the time, day in and day out. On that morning, I looked into her eyes after getting this news and I just felt compelled to apologize. We wound up building a friendship and that was a life-changing moment for me.

Being locked up taught me survival skills, but nobody should have to use these skills to survive. So I work as a youth organizer for the Prison Moratorium Project. I do workshops and trainings around the youth and juvenile justice system. I distribute information around the prison-industrial complex to the people who are most affected by it. And hopefully they are inspired to act on it. Even if they don't act on it in an organized way, they can act on it in their life. Maybe they will make life decisions that will not put them and those they love in jail.

I also break down the lies that we have been given by the media about why the government justifies the building of so many juvenile prisons. I encourage them to get at the root cause of why this violence exists.

❹ What are the messages that young women in this society receive around violence?

We get a lot of mixed messages: Violence begets violence, if someone hits you hit them back, call the police, don't call the police. We are told that if we get our asses beat or if we are emotionally abused, it's OK. We probably deserved it, and if it's not OK, don't worry, the authorities will lock you up or they will lock up the person who is doing it to you.

Humans are the most violent beings on the planet because we are driven by our emotions and because our emotions have been so manipulated and distorted we have very little control over them. Young women are not immune to this. We condone violence collectively as a nation and then attempt to condemn it on an individual level. Our world is not peaceful, so how can we be peaceful?

❺ Is the conversation about violence personal or political? Why?

Both, for me, because the political affects my personal and my personal affects my interpersonal. Why? Because nothing is separate; nothing is black and white, it is all interconnected and I can't just work on one limb of violence when the whole body is hurting. We as a society never deal with the root cause. There is always a big picture even in the most personal cases of interpersonal violence; it is always precipitated by some larger environmental factor.

I am a violent person, but my politics are about peace. But I don't think there will be a peaceful journey getting to that peace. Regardless of how I feel, I won't go in a store with a gun and shoot people. I have to be real about my efforts to know that what I am fighting has bigger guns than I do. I am a product of the system trying to fight the system. My politics are always changing evolving and growing; I have to change grow and evolve with them. Sometimes I get frustrated with organizing because I don't always get the results I want. But I have to believe that in some way my efforts matter.

Me and my people are often not even on the same page about what it will take and so we wind up fighting each other. I am half white, but I hated white people. But now that I have traveled and seen different people and places I have to grow beyond that. I hate white imperialism, I hate oppression, I hate racism.

Even white activists still play out cracker bullshit. But I try to examine the root on a case-by-case basis. Sometimes I have to put my everyday politics to the side, especially in relationships, because my life may not always fit my politics.

❻ What do you think are the most common types of violence affecting young women?

Personally, I am caught up in the mental violence. Sometimes I have physical confrontations, but the most devastating violence I face is mental. Being a queer women of color, I try to navigate this straight world with a broken compass; I feel like I get lost.

We as young women are most commonly affected by mental violence because we are always being pressured to be something we are not, be it white, skinny, blonde, and so on. We tan and bleach our skin, cut ourselves; we physically destroy our bodies and we destroy our minds by making ourselves believe that this is good for us. The result is that we corrupt our soul, and if our soul is corrupted, how can we possibly be at peace?

❼ Why do you think more women are joining the military?

Lack of resources, lack of opportunities—many women join to survive. However, the military does not publish how many women get raped in these institutions, and that the rules are very different from civilian society. No matter how much they tell us that things are changing, it continues to be a male-dominated environment. We get fed the basic set of ideas and are fooled into believing it will be different. Sometimes we are joining because we want to be patriotic and sometimes we just do it for the money. But we have to understand, taking care of ourselves is the most patriotic thing we can do.

For some of us, we really need to feel a part of something and we feel compelled to show our strength because we are tired of being seen as the victim.

❽ How can women individually and collectively work to end the cycle of violence in their own lives?

We must install some honor, respect, and morals. There is no honor no more. There used to be respect; even in street life there were rules and honor. I feel like I got to get on the same page with my sisters and realize there is no end to what we can do, but as long as we are at odds with each other it will not change.

We need more role models and positive examples. Women of color particularly in this country do not have this. Zapatista women, now those are examples of strong, passionate, committed women, but we don't get to have access to them, we don't have women in our community who are lifted up. We need powerful women to step up more and consciously be willing to take on being an example.

My grandmother—she took care of all of it. She dealt with me even though she was in her sixties when I was born. If I have a tenth of her strength, I can do it. Even though my mother was living the drug life, she was strong. I watched her wrestle cops to the floor and beat the dudes up. The women in my family are strong. I feel like that shit is in my blood.

My greatest role model now is an Asian woman, which is bigger than my politics of living in Brooklyn and clashing with the Korean retail community. That this Korean woman can now be my mentor, shows *my growth*. We need to be willing to step beyond what we know for that mentorship and support. It may be scary, but if anything, it's worth it—if not just for the adventure alone.

We don't have to look too far, and we don't need to put each other on high-expectation pedestals. It could be your auntie who struggled with drugs and finally got her shit together—that's dope man, you know what I'm sayin'!?

My Return

by Nicole Goodwin

The hardest part of war is that there will never be any words written that will truly describe its carnage or its legacy to the world. That has been the uphill struggle that I have had to face for the past two years.

Most of the world sees the "war on terror" through the eyes and the ears of the news. Yet underneath the constant chaos that is brought to you through local media is the untold story of the soldiers on the battlefield. The most complicated thing for me to say about myself is that I was in Iraq for four months, and yet my soul has never really left the desert. That kind of experience cannot be shaken off as easily as the U.S. government would have you believe, whether or not we are the victors in the end.

My unit lived across the street from a Coalition police station. I witnessed one car bombing and too many shootouts between the police and the insurgents to count. But it was more dangerous for us when we were in transit. In fact, I stopped going on missions with my unit because my captain almost got the convoy I was in trapped in an ambush! The captain decided to take the scenic route around the city just to get to Martyr's Monument, where our battalion was stationed. The attack started fifteen minutes after our arrival and lasted for three hours.

Even though I was stationed in Iraq, I was blessed to never have fired my weapon. There, I learned that there are many forms of beauty—the way the stars revealed to me a glimpse of heaven every night. I learned that even in the mists of hell, heaven is not so far away.

I suppose the truth that a place like that unveils can destroy anyone's concept of the word "atrocity."

It's hard to believe that I was there at all. But my memories are vivid still: the debris that was placed where buildings, shops, and people once stood; the constant view of wreckage everyday the sun came up; houses blown apart with families still living in them; no running water to take a bath, let alone a shower more than once a day. I will never forget.

Nicole Goodwin *is a twenty-five-year-old black student who recently returned from fighting in Iraq.*

I wanted to tell them that they were wrong, that vanilla milkshakes smell like Clorox the day after, that hands push hard on the backs of heads, hard enough for you to gag, that the skin on the inside of your throat is more delicate than the space between your legs and both can bleed if pressed too hard. That even if they fill the empty places in your body, it's no guarantee that you will be filled.

—Lisa Ascalon, "Easy"

Domesticated Brutality

by Hilda Herrera
from the We Got Issues! Performance Piece

There underneath the paleness of her skin was the evidence of his
abusive nature.
A rainbow of black and blue broken capillaries that bled painfully
every time she attempted to smile.
She had a doctorate in cosmetology. Covering up the traces was her
expertise.
He was a cop, his insecurities hidden in the same wallet where he
kept his shield.
His semiautomatic weapon was the affirmation of his masculinity:
the man that he wished his father would have taught him to be.

She used to reminisce of the times before the war.
The times before the touch of his hands created agony.
When they used to love each other
When she would lie by his side, and his divine presence would make
her travel the world way before the sun could rise and create a
new dawn.
When he was mesmerized by the intensive light of her existence.

Six months into her pregnancy
He placed his hands around her neck and slammed her against the
wall,

rationalizing his actions with idiotic statements:

"Look what you made me do to you."

"If you weren't so slick at the mouth, I wouldn't be so quick with
   the hands."

She became a victim because that was just what her mother would do.

He pulled his gun from the closet and shoved it in her face.

Her taste buds kept regurgitating the lead particles that deposited
   in her mouth.

She begged him time and time again to pull the trigger—but he
   didn't have the *cojones* for that.

When he and the baby fell asleep

she went into the closet where he hid his gun, and, if not for the
   sudden cry of her son,

he would now be a name on a tombstone and she a number in the
   state pen.

Hilda Herrera *is an urban Cuban-American poet and spoken-word*
artist who lives in New York City.

You have not cried in vain, mujer
for I will chant your cries
Retell your story to my babies
Your legacy of *shine*
—Gabriela Erandi Rico, "Shine"

since my body

by Kay Barrett

i am no wooden doorframe
watching you walk away again.

i am dwelling on lumbered
voice, octaves trying to carve out a
full night of sleep.

can i write that poem?
(propping up metaphors to disconnect the skin cells)
can i write that poem?
the *quiet, hold still*—the *i am*
trembling, stop it, no no—or

do i count on the ceiling
to keep me from screaming out of this room?

this is not sound-bite comfort to a survivor
or a diligent response to your alcohol
breath and suctioned hands:
lover gone bad,
lover does not punch but—,
lover circles a body closer closer until it drains,
lover demand demand demands until empty,
. . . lover?

i want to warn the rest.
tell them
your hands are malice and have the
coldness of x's.

      your hands erase.
i now hate my bed.

turning my belly to the mattress,
i wonder if i had not the spine,
where would the rest of me be?

your hands would
have taken me apart / your tongue a shelf,
packing the arms / the thighs /
the obtuse of my
ear /
for re-occurring nightmares

and when do i let myself alive again?
after a new girl kisses my forehead?
will she bathe me her armskin, take her hands and
place them on cheek,
let me take the lead?

will i push until intimacy walks out on me?
until all i am left with are my own hands
and lofty deep sounds? until i massage out
the welts you left with coffee at 2 a.m. and
another poem that will never be read aloud?

do you think that i am made of vacant corners?
am i not supposed to
open up my sunken heart? not
for the life in me dare another woman

on these collarbones?

you do not mark that easy.
no territory of my map has your lines clearly drawn.
my dirt, my growing, my mass, my direction
my daring, my breathtaking
were never yours.

the colonizer in you,
the arrogance in you
that claims that:

    this was nothing at all,

is questioning at night.
is lampshade light monitoring the folds of the hand.
is sick of every movement
since my body.

Kay Barrett *is a twenty-four-year-old Filipina/Pinay hapa queer teaching artist who lives in Chicago.*

rant
sometimes when you fight so hard

by Kelly Zen-Yie Tsai

settle down little sister
speak love little sister

i know you are a queen

sister queen
sister queen

the dogs aren't gonna bite you
this world wasn't made to fight you
and reality stings like a muthafucka
if you know what i mean

and there's nothing we can grab
with our angry hands
unless
we kill it
   conquer it
      possess it
         and then it's not really ours
            and then it's already dead

but breathe breathe
little sister

take it slow little sister
let it go little sister

and let your lungs expand beneath
your bones little sister

you don't have to let any fingers touch you
no pads of prints to soften your skin
no knuckles exploring your ribbons
no fists tearing at your clothes

you don't have to fight or recognize
you don't have to open or close your eyes here

breathe breathe little sister
love love little sister

love so hard
until you can let go

love so hard
until your heart
splits in two
one juicy muscle
and one rotten flap
choking on the blood
that pumps through you
like a waterfall
with ambition
for better days
     better things

give give little sister
yourself time in front of the mirror

with no one over your shoulder
no god, no spirit, no ghost

no gun muzzle pointing
or blade held to your neck

no girl cackling back
who can hurt the most
breathe breathe
little sister
give give
little sister

and know
that the existence
of opposition
in this world
is truly
false

Kelly Zen-Yie Tsai *is a Chinese-Taiwanese-American spoken word and multidisciplinary theater artist based in Brooklyn and Chicago.*

Baby girl never gets a complete embrace
from her father because it's lost
in the sand of Iraq.
—Chivonnie Letiea, "In the Sand of Iraq"

Gun Control

by Sara Littlecrow Russell
from the We Got Issues! Performance Piece

Owning a gun is the ultimate feminism. Men don't know what it's like to walk down the street and to be afraid. Women, they have to be afraid all the time to survive.

Me? I'm sick of it. Sick of not being able to wear high heels on the subway because I can't run in them.

I just want to be free to be a woman. A woman unafraid. So I carry a gun. A big gun. And I know how to use it, too. Now I can enjoy a hike or even a skinny dip in the woods without worrying about the sound of every snapping twig. When I go out, I'm no longer afraid to be as sexy as I want to be, because I know that I won't get raped. Men respect a woman with a gun. Men listen to a woman with a gun.

In fact, I bet we'd be a hell of a lot closer to world peace if humanitarian relief meant that every woman in the world was packing a gun on her hip. Just imagine, refugee camps full of .357-strapped African women—no more aid workers forcing them to give blow jobs for a bag of rice. Imagine Afghani women packing AK-47 under their veils—I bet the Taliban would think twice about tearing their clothes off. Imagine Thai mothers with 9 millimeters, who'd come and steal their daughters and sons for the sex trade?

Sara Littlecrow Russell is a Native American activist and award-winning playwright. "Gun Control" is part of the WGI! Performance Piece.

In Memory of March 5, 2004

by Meghan Collins

Oh my.
For today is the second anniversary of my incarceration.
And I drank sufficiently, and continue the drinking here at home.
Where I belong. :)
Big ups to the blue drink and the waitress named Sarah. And for her
getting me a half dozen of them. :)
And steak. I love steak

Someone told me today that I am not the same person as I was when
I went into jail. I'm not. The same person also told me that I am no
fun anymore, that I don't go out and party anymore or anything like
that. Of course I don't. If you had seen the sights I saw, you would
understand. Four months in jail might not seem like much to some.

Of all the experiences in my life so far, I took the most from this one.
I walked away, out of the fucking tunnel, into the real world—and I
was afraid. Because I've seen what prison can do to a person. I've
seen what life really is. I've seen what life can make you do as a
means of escape. I've seen so much, for someone so young.

Two years ago today, I was in a cell. I was in a fucking sack, made out
of cheap fabric and minimal padding, lying on a mat on the cold, cold
floor, wondering what I'd done to deserve what I was getting. I had
no socks, no shoes, no underwear. I couldn't tie my hair back. I was

reduced to nothing. The cheap fabric sack scratched my skin and the Velcro wouldn't hold anymore, after years of misuse.

My number was 140362. I will never forget that number.

I will never forget watching a woman kick dope and vomit profusely, in the toilet and on herself, with six teeth in her mouth and holes in her arms, while shivering in the cold that March can produce. I cried for myself. I cried for what I'd left behind. I cried to my father, a year cold in the ground, that he in his own way, would somehow save me from this torture.

I cried with my mother in a three-by-three room with glass separating us. I was so hysterical I couldn't get it across to her the pain that I felt. I held my hand up to the glass, and she held up hers, and we both cried tears of shame, tears of sorrow, and tears of loss. We were separated by silicone, pushed apart by situation.

I cried for the girl who, two years prior, had gotten behind the wheel, after watching a national treasure crumble spinelessly on the ground, had made the choice to drink three beers and drive home.

I never made it home.
I wonder now if I ever did.

And you wonder if I ever took anything from my experience. You wonder, looking at me drinking my screwdriver and chain smoking, with Xanax in my hand and a dream in my heart, if I ever learned from my mistakes?

Look deeper, and wonder if there's anything that I did not see. Wonder if there is anything that I did not feel. Every emotion, amplified by cinder-block walls and wool blankets, see-through socks and soul-seeking conversations down a toilet bowl, I felt every fucking emotion while I sat there by myself in that twelfth-floor pod. In four short months, I experienced anything that nay grown, good person had ever felt, ever suffered—even more so.

Simultaneous joy and pain seeing the one person you love, but not being able to just feel the texture of the palm against yours through that glass. That partition. That hateful glass. Going back to your bunk and crying for hours because you know full well that it will never be the same. Ever. I had four months of my life stripped from me. Stolen, because of poor choice. Ripped away in an act of idiocy, and all I can say is, I did this to myself.

First and foremost, I did this to myself. And I can never truly go home again.

Meghan Collins *is a photographer, model, and poet.*

I Should Never Have Written This Down but I Can't Bear to Tear It Down

by Sage Fisher

I should never have written this down but I can't bear to tear it
out.

So you know that unfortunate feeling when you're alone in the woods
with someone you don't want to be there with and you've had
some drinks and you realize you're just miserable? And all that
would help is 1) being fucked, even against your will or 2) severe
pain (i.e., cutting) and/or death or 3) more alcohol. And you're
just mad at yourself because you shouldn't have drank and you
knew it was going to happen, you fucking knew better! So you
tell yourself you're never drinking again (like always and the last
time and the time before that) but at the same time you realize
that this is, sadly, the only true emotion, it's called life, all knotted up with love and hate and pain and crickets that won't shut
up and bad poetry despite the lame attempts and the music is
too soft or too loud and someone is trying to kiss you but you
can't stop thinking about your ex and you know you hate yourself and the world but you feel some intense love for someone or
something you most definitely cannot recall and you find yourself alone in the dark in your car writing it all down on paper as
evidence so that people can know just how pathetic you are (but

also realize that you are right on, and that at another point in
their life they were you and they feel your pain and want to
watch from a distance and wince with you when you bleed and
whisper don't do that, no, no, when you let him kiss you).
Goodnight, dream sweet,
you are nothing.
The world is too big and too beautiful, it brings tears to the corners of
your eyes
so when you wake
you can wipe off the sleep
and be glad
you can't remember what reality tastes like.

*Sage Fisher has been writing since she was old enough to think, drawing
since she was old enough to hold a pencil, and writing songs since she realized music is the best way to reach people. She is from Hawaii.*

rant
what are we teaching our daughters

by Allison Joy

he was a bold criminal.
all his offenses took place in the daylight
under the least of suspicions,
his felonies cloaked
by the so-called innocence
of youth.

but behind those bushes
and under the multicolored
tent made of bedsheets,
in the stale air of the basement
they would play games,
and he made the rules.
games are sometimes
one-sided.

there are so many like him,
who escape punishment
because they are supposedly so safe.
fathers, brothers, uncles, and friends—
what a kind and gentle man to insist upon
tucking a child in to sleep,
or taking the day off
to baby-sit.

girls pretend it's not happening.
they close their eyes
or stare at the ceiling,

make note of the number of leaves
there are on the branch of the tree
right outside the window.
they concentrate on other things,
the smell of lunch cooking downstairs
in the kitchen,
the chirping of summer tree frogs,
sounds of midday traffic.

when it's done they button up
and zip up
and tidy up
and curl up to sleep.

to escape.

they smile big smiles,
play sports,
go to church,
and do well in school.

to escape.

my,
what a beautiful young woman,
people say.

girls always bear the burden
of feeling guilty.
as if their pristine purity
has become stained
due to their own accord,
led to believe
they have dirtied themselves
through no one's fault but their own.

what are we teaching our daughters?
their secrets are strangled by shame
so they suffer in silence.

it is a pity we don't teach our daughters early
how to fight.

instead of ballet lessons,
perhaps kickboxing is more suited
for them in this world,
where society tells them to lie submissive,
too afraid to cry
or even whisper
what screams in their heads—

no.

Allison Joy is currently a performer in the We Got Issues! National tour, and makes damn good spicy brownies. This queer Filipina American believes in the strength of her sisters, community building, art as activism, grassroots organizing, loving honestly, linking arms with all oppressed peoples, and manifesting visions of liberation.

His mentality remained caged
Displacing his rage on his children,
his women, and his music
He loved them so hard it was even
harder not to abuse them.
—Hilda Herrera, "Martyrs of a Lamppost"

Ritual of Empowerment

Aura Cleanse

Sit quietly. Imagine a root or light coming from the base of the spine going deep into the ground. Think about the issue or problem that needs to be removed and/or cleansed. Imagine that you are sending the energy of that issue down into the earth. Ask that the energy be recycled.

It is very important that the cleansed space be filled with positive energy. Try imagining sunlight coming in through the crown of your head and filling your aura.

Release

This ritual is best done with a community of sisters. You'll need:
• Punching bags or big pillows
• A private, outdoor area

Have your sisters stand around you in a circle holding the punching bags or pillows. One person says your name and asks, "What do you want to release?"

Name what you want to let go of. Punch and kick every single pillow until you can't punch or kick anymore.

Allow yourself to feel what comes up: *cry* it out; *scream* it out; *punch and kick it out!*

Release that negative energy that is creating barriers in your life.

When you're done, your sisters should come in together, hold you, and offer you good wishes.

We Got Stats!

➡ The **"war on drugs" is increasingly targeting women,** who are being arrested and prosecuted for nonviolent, drug-related offenses. The rate of increase of imprisonment of women for drug crime has outpaced men. —American Civil Liberties Union (2005)

➡ More than **1 million women** are under the control of the criminal justice system. —American Civil Liberties Union (2005)

➡ **Every 9 seconds a woman is beaten in the United States.**
—American Institute on Domestic Violence

➡ The Central Intelligence Agency estimates that **between 50,000 and 100,000 women are trafficked into the United States** each year, mostly for the purposes of commercial sexual exploitation. —Amy O'Neill Richard. U.S. Department of State

➡ Domestic violence occurs in **18% of lesbian relationships** in the U.S. —Wikipedia

➡ **Immigrant women are less likely to leave their abusers for fear of deportation.** 72.3% of the battered Latinas surveyed reported that their spouses never filed immigration petitions for their wives even though 50.8% of the victims qualified to have petitions filed on their behalf.

—M. A. Dutton, L. E. Orloff, and G. Aguilar Hass. *Georgetown Journal on Poverty Law & Publicity* (2000)

➡ **78% of women in prison have children.**
—Steven R. Donzinger, *The Real War on Crime* (1996)

➡ Every year approximately 132,000 women report that they have been victims of rape or attempted rape, and more than half of them knew their attackers. **It's estimated that 2 to 6 times that many women are raped, but do not report it.** —National Organization for Women

➡ The number of women committing violent acts have increased in the latter half of the 20th century. Women have the natural capacity to be as violent as men; the difference is that **women need greater incentives to express that violence.** —Barry Yeoman, *Psychology Today* (1999)

➡ **The risks of handgun ownership far outweigh the benefits.** In 2000, for every 1 time a woman used a handgun to kill a stranger in self-defense, 222 women were murdered in handgun homicides. —Violence Policy Center

Chapter 8

Got Money?
Adventures in Abundance

Now, I ain't sayin she a gold-digger . . .

—Kanye West

Rha Rants

My mother used to have a saying, "Every good rat has more than one hole to crawl into," which was her way of saying always keep your options open and always cover your ass.

Born with a natural poker face, my mother weaved an impenetrable web of secrecy around money; she'd pull rabbits out of hats and dollars out of bras or stockings in the most desperate times. My parents, like the rest of America who discovered credit cards and loans in the mid-'60s, lived way beyond their means. At an early age I, too, learned how to put on a poker face when it came to dealing with the butcher, the baker, and the candlestick maker.

Liz Perle, in *Money, a Memoir: Women, Emotions, and Cash,* calls this culture of overaspiring and overspending the Emotional Middle Class. Perle brilliantly explains how the postwar economy, two-income households, and the brand-name sale of the American dream has taken our society into the spending stratosphere with plenty of plastic to help soften the ride.

The myth of fabulousness is so alluring; I mean, who wouldn't want to be pampered and catered to all the time? Everything on TV looks so clean and shiny, and people are always smiling, smiling, smiling, with awesome tans and perfect teeth. The problem, as Perle explains, is that we learn to view this excessive, possessive culture as normal, and we come to believe that we're *entitled* to live this way, whether our bank account agrees with us or not.

Two years ago, I vowed that I was going to resolve my issues around money—aka "I ain't gonna be broke no more"—but what I've discovered, shockingly, is that how much money I have or don't have isn't really the issue. The emotions I've attached to them are what's kicking my butt.

Is it OK for me to want? Is there such a thing as healthy aspiration? Or am I just an all-day sucker for the global mass-marketing machine? I am definitely one of those people who has seen herself as Ms. Nonmaterialistic. Artists and activists have sung antiestablishment anthems of starvation from the beginning of time, but, I've also turned up my nose at struggling, declaring that bread and water is neither something I can nor want to pledge my allegiance to.

These conflicting philosophies have landed me all over the map; my money freestyle has swung me in and out of debt while keeping me firmly rooted in denial. Yes, I am an *avoider* and most definitely a card-carrying member of the EMC. Gee, I wonder where I got that from?

Growing up, when money was low, my mother and father would announce, "Things are tight." Electricity would be turned off; we kids would be forced to answer the phone and take messages and anytime the bell rang, we would all duck down, with one of us sent to the window above the front door to see who it was. Not even two days later, my mother would burst through the door, carrying bags and beaming, beckoning my sister and me to be the audience for her own private fashion show. Every so often, she would excitedly throw something our way; "Try this on!"

These mixed messages created years of fiscal irresponsibility on my part and as much as I shunned my parents in my early professional years, when the going got tough, I went into survival mode, with "every good rat . . ." echoing in the distance.

I'm finally coming to explore the idea of *enough*. Coming clean about my aspirations one skeleton at a time has given me the courage to ask myself: What do I *really* need? What are the most important things to me right now? Is more really better? Is it OK *not* to want? How can I express my gratitude for what I already have?

The concept of scarcity in this society continues to have devastating effects on the hearts, minds, and spirits of so many of us. Anytime I feel constricted or out of control around money I ask myself, What is this really about? I have been amazed at how often it has been more about mental, emotional, and spiritual freedom—*not* about the cash.

In the words of money expert Barbara Stanley: "It's not about money; it's about power. Taking financial responsibility and becoming financially independent is a rite of passage into our power. I really do believe that power demands that we become responsible adults—the ultimate authority in our lives—and money enables us to do that. I think we are scared of the power. Power demands that we stand up and think and act for ourselves. It demands that we take up space, that we value ourselves."

I agree.

We are so in debt with the cost of America's "middle-class" reality that we can't even afford our own morals and values.
—Rha Goddess, "ENOUGH!"

Empowered

Natalie Doel

Natalie Dole was born and raised in Maine and went to college in Philadelphia, where exposure to people with different backgrounds led her to think deeply about the role of privilege in personal and political development. Her focus has shifted from the strictly scientific approach to exploring the social aspects of the challenges facing the planet today. She lives in San Francisco and is a development assistant with the Pachamama Alliance (www.pachamama.org), a nonprofit whose mission is the creation of an environmentally sustainable, spiritually fulfilling, and socially just human presence on this planet.

Age:
26
Cultural Identity:
Born a WASP, consciously evolving
Born:
In Maine
Education:
BA in biology and environmental sciences, Bryn Mawr College
Occupation:
Fundraising in the social profit (aka nonprofit) sector
Economic Class:
Upper middle
Marital Status:
Single
Registered to vote:
Yes, with the Green Party

❶ How would you describe your relationship with money now? What has been most influential in shaping it?

I now take very seriously the task of increasing the consciousness of my consumption patterns. I'm very blessed not to have any immediate money concerns, and this gives me the freedom to think of it primarily as an expression of my values and a way to build the world I want to be a part of. I would say that my relationship to money has been totally transformed recently by my contact with Lynne Twist, author of *The Soul of Money*. I urge anyone who is struggling to redefine their relationship with money to read that book. Even better, partner with someone else to discuss the ideas it contains and brainstorm ways to put those ideas into practice. Transformation loves company.

❷ Why did you decide to work in the area of money?

I felt called to a career in nonprofit fundraising after attending Lynne Twist's Fundraising from the Heart workshop following last year's Bioneers conference (www.bioneers.org). I was inspired by the idea that fundraisers perform a sacred role by helping people reconnect with their values, whether they end up giving or not. The importance of "taking a stand" was emphasized, because it gives you a power that transcends taking a "position," and gives others space to empower themselves. I loved the idea that even if someone isn't ready to give you money, just by interacting with them you may have helped open them up to the possibility of giving *somewhere*. When Lynne said that we're trying to "expand the pie, not just carve it up differently," I was hooked.

❸ Is being financially secure only tied to how much money you have? Why or why not?

I feel particularly qualified to answer this question because of a financial serendipity that I was blessed with three years ago. Before it happened, I was so preoccupied with getting a job and paying off school loans that I neglected the one thing that I most needed to do: define who I was. I had only a vague idea of where my life was going, and the sense that I would never have time to figure it out filled me with despair. After the windfall, I finally felt free to travel and pursue a very nonlinear professional path, and this has led me to greater fulfillment today than I could have dreamed of before. But what I've come to realize is that the money itself was really only a small part of what made that possible. The real liberation was from a very narrow concept of what constitutes financial security. I realized that I could have done it even without my windfall: It just would have taken more creativity and less risk-aversion. The point is that broadening our concept of financial security can create as much personal freedom as the kind of windfall I received.

❹ What do you think are the top three mental barriers to achieving financial security?

I believe that all barriers to financial security are primarily mental. I would point first to a mistaken belief, very deeply rooted in our worldview, that happiness lies outside of ourselves. The materialistic culture we grow up in teaches us from a very early age that our only real value is as consumers—this is constantly reinforced by advertising. The second barrier, also deeply ingrained, is the idea that more is always better, that "more" in fact defines "progress." Out-of-control consumerism causes us to attach so much of our personal value to our possessions that in the end it is they that possess us. Finally, I think people often feel very isolated in their financial struggles, because there is a strong stigma attached to being in debt or not being "rich." This must change; people must find ways to support each other in their quest for financial security, and women will undoubtedly blaze this trail.

❺ What can we do to change our limiting perceptions and become empowered in our ability to handle our money?

Controlling our finances is in large part a question of examining the strategies we use to meet not only material needs, but emotional ones as well. Carve out some time alone so you can focus on what needs you are trying to meet with spending that you might be able to meet more effectively in other ways. It's especially helpful to examine our notions of self-interest. Is self-interest synonymous with selfishness, or will using your money to better your community do more for your well-being than paying fifty dollars a month for cable? This kind of thinking gets easier with practice, so don't be intimidated!

❻ How can putting our money where are hearts are, i.e., toward good causes, further our ability to have financial security?

No matter how great or small your wealth, you alone have *complete control* over how you spend it. Even if most of your income goes toward basic needs, by carefully planning your expenditures and thinking deeply about what is really important, almost anyone can carve out a sum that they can donate regularly to the cause of her choice. You can start down the path of conscious consumerism with very small changes. As these add up over time, we find that "divine reallocation" puts us so in touch with the difference between wants and needs that financial stability follows almost effortlessly. The spiritual nourishment we derive from putting our money to work for our values fills to overflowing the void that we had tried to fill unsuccessfully before with frivolous purchases.

Money, in many ways, defines our lives, and that means it is perhaps the single most important vehicle that we have to effect change.

Circular Money Rant (or, It's Damn Hard to Break Free of Shit)

by Jennifer Cendaña Armas

1/29/06

Dear God,

You've been put on notice. *For real* this time.

Why make me beg for extra dollars in my pocket even more than I already have?

I've prayed, worked jobs I've loved and not loved all hours of the day and night.

I've given offerings of fruit and liquor, sung and danced in worship, pinched pennies 'til I bled, spent dollars I didn't have believing it would return to me threefold, read books, written poems, cast spells, lit candles, chanted positive affirmations.

And then I worked more with nothing else in my pay stub.

Days are safe in struggle—a safety I need destroyed. It's brought nothing but tiredness and routine. All I have to mark my labor are knotted hands and pinched nerves in my lower back.

What else do you need before I can take what is mine?

I have nothing more to give.

2/2/06

Dear Goddess,

Goddess bless you for listening. Thank you for this check in my hand.

(Forget everything I said a few days ago. Please don't hold it against me, Almighty.)

In thanks for these blessings, I will light several candles in the name of Lazarus, who rose from the dead like my savings this day.

All praises.

2/25/06
No more notice.

God—fuck you.

Jennifer Cendaña Armas is a multiethnic, multiracial, self-loving, balanced supastar creator from Corona/Jackson Heights, Queens, forever-traveling the world.

rant

what we will have when we have enough

by Kelly Zen-Yie Tsai

morning
exploded
from silence

      cloudburst

down came
the plates

broken
smashed

one ceramic shard
flew

and nicked
the youngest
daughter's cheek

mother cried at the table
as father packed his bags

a morning of pancakes
      applesauce
      and syrup

straight out of the
mickey mouse cookbook

        money
           somethin'
about money

the twenty-year-old
christmas tree

they bought
when they first
came to the u.s.

leaned against
the living room wall

    painted wooden stick
    stuck with color-coded branches
    twisted green wire

it followed them
for two decades more

from the cul de sac
bursting with immigrants

to the subdivision
power-walked by soccer moms

to the village
hushed by the senator,
psychiatrists, and restauranteurs

       money
          somethin'
about money

the eldest wears
two beepers on her belt

carries one cell phone
     one blackberry

climbs the hills
of dot-com busted
san francisco

whenever
wherever

a computer
shuts down

she is called to work

we are very
creative people

she reminds herself

we are surrounded
by creativity
        money
           somethin'
about money

the youngest
lays on a futon
in brooklyn

counts her dollars
from last night's
open mic

glances at taped cutouts
thumbtacked into her wall

    chaka khan
    basquiat
    etheridge knight
    bei dao

she rolls her dollars
into a ball

stuffs them
in a cardboard box

turns out the light

finally
she says

enough

Kelly Zen-Yie Tsai *is a Chinese-Taiwanese-American spoken word and multidisciplinary theater artist based in Brooklyn and Chicago.*

Greedy conglomerates study our culture, only to learn more ways to market and exploit it. The rap industry makes billions of dollars, but despite what the rented cars, clothes, and cribs in the videos imply, the pockets of the creators remain empty.
—JLove, "The Future of Hip-Hop"

Anyone can get paid money and consider herself "rich," but not too many can actually become wealthy. Wealth is acquired through knowledge, not only knowledge of self, but knowledge of circumstance and knowledge of priority. Then and only then will you be truly rich.

—Pri the Honey Dark, artist

Money Sickness

by Lea Endres

I am so, so sick of not having money or more accurately, not having enough money to cover the expenses of living even a very, very, very simple, nonconsumer-based lifestyle in this country.

I am sick of counting pennies, of writing checks that I know will bounce if I don't get my paycheck deposited in time.

I am sick of rushing to the bank to deposit those paychecks and sick of knowing that the money is allocated before it's even in my back account.

I am fucking sick of not signing up for yoga classes because I don't have the money and sick of *not* buying health insurance because I don't have the money.

I am sick of money I am sick of money I am sick of money.

I am sick of seeing people with money look like they own the world, thinking that things should move out of the way for them, sick of seeing shiny, polished made-up faces with the latest designer lip gloss sticking their noses up at the poor people who pass them on the streets.

I am sick of wanting money, of wanting something I don't have, of dreaming of traveling but not being able to, of having a book I want on a list for two months but not having the money to buy it.

I am sick of random unconscious splurges on four-dollar organic smoothies that I "need" in order to stay sane, but that then deplete my reserves instantaneously.

I am sick of feeling worthless and less-than and dirty when I pull my dented 1994 Mazda Protégé up next to a new BMW with the owner either not looking in my direction because I am not worth the glance, or looking at me with a mixture of pity and amusement.

I am sick of feeling two-inches tall under this gaze.

I am sick of walking past heavily cologned men in business suits and feeling like I am wearing a trash bag because my jeans are well worn and my shoes are scuffed hand-me-downs.

I am sick of feeling really privileged and really poor at the same time.

I am sick of borrowing money from my loved ones in times of need.

I am sick of compulsively calling my bank at all hours of the day to double check the transactions that I've listed in my check register to make sure I haven't missed something that will put me in the negative.

I am sick of calling and learning that I went under by thirty-five cents and my bank has charged me a thirty-dollar non-sufficient funds fee, making the new balance negative thirty dollars and thirty-five cents.

I am sick of crying on the occasion that I get a parking ticket because I know that I can't pay the thirty-five or forty dollars, and by the time I will be able to pay it, the ticket will have increased to ninety dollars.

I am so sick of thinking about money every single day of my life, and associating my worth in the world with a fictitious digital entity that is not even tied to the gold standard anymore.

I am so sick of feeling less-than and not worthy in the face of a well-groomed, perfect-toothed smiling man who makes a living standing on the backs of other people.

I am tired of feeling like a victim and acting like a victim when it comes to this insane capitalistic money-centered society.

I am sick of thinking that $40,000 will solve all my problems because it will pay off my student loans and my debt to the credit card company and to my dad.

I am so sick of being in debt, sick of being indebted, sick of the entire concept of debt.

I am so sick of the cycle of poverty, of being in the exact same place that I was in ten years ago, and sick of knowing that it's all me—

knowing that it's my own unhealthy relationship to money
that is causing it all.

Lea Endres is a human rights educator and artist finally reclaiming her own right to personal and economic health. She is currently living in Los Angeles.

A Little Girl's Song

by Marla Teyolia

Little girl
Little girl
Too young to count pennies
Little girl
Little girl
Thought her family had plenty
'Till her mama made her call her dad on the phone
Asking him for child support
She feels all alone
He says rude things and hangs up the phone
Little girl
Little girl
Can hear her heart moan

Little girl
Little girl
Sees her mom working hard
Her brothers take and take
Livin' high on the hog
"mama give me this"
"mama give me that"
they spend all her money
spend half of it on crack

Little girl grows up
gets a Little man
rich Jewish boy from the Promised Land
promises her diamonds
even gives her pearls
takes her on a cruise all around the world
Mama thinks he's lovely—oh, he is a keepa'!
Friends try to stop her pockets from getting deepa'

Little girl
Little girl
Tries hard to break free
Searches for abundance and divinity

Little girl grows up and gets a little stronger
Her vision of prosperity gets a little broader

Love
Health
Family and
Friends . . .
Little girl, Little girl
Needs *them* to no end

But let's not forget about the big ol' scrilla
Little girl, Little girl
Dreams her pockets bigga'

Ain't nothing wrong with money
Of this there's no doubt
She's learned not to chase it
But to live her dreams out

Money and righteousness
in the same place?

Damn right'!
'cuz
this Little girl
has a life
to create!

Marla Teyolia, actor, writer, all-around diva, loves life, laughter, making dinner with her husband, chilling with her girls, walking her dogs, and just being in the presence of the ocean.

It is true that you cannot get something for nothing. You must give to make way to receive. The law also works the other way: You cannot give anything without getting something for it. Give the best you have and then look for the best in return. This is the law of receiving.
—Catherine Ponder, *Secret of Unlimited Prosperity*

Ritual of Empowerment

A Money Herstory

Each of us has a herstory with money, built from messages we've gotten from family, loved ones, friends, teachers, bosses, and mentors, as well as larger societal forces such as TV, movies, other media, and advertising.

Coleen Trimble, in her phenomenal seminar called the Heart of Money, encourages all of her participants to create a money biography; deeply inspired by this work, we encourage young women to create a money herstory. We often dream of being financially secure or maybe even rich. However, part of our greatest empowerment as young women lies in our ability to confront and embrace our current reality, and the beliefs and attitudes that feed it.

This exercise will take anywhere from forty-five minutes to an hour. Use your journal if you have one; however, any clean sheets of paper will suffice. Find a comfortable, quiet space where you won't be disturbed.

Money herstory questions:
- What are your earliest memories concerning money?
- What are the strongest messages you received about money while growing up (from your mother, your father, other family members, and/or other people)?

- How would you describe your family's relationship to money? Did they have money? Where they poor? What did they believe about money? How did they behave as a result of those beliefs?
- When and how did you begin to interact with societal norms around money (e.g., the attitudes and beliefs surrounding the image of success and what it takes to be successful)?
- How are your own attitudes and beliefs about money shaped by your parents and family? By current societal norms? By other internal and external influences?
- How are your own attitudes and beliefs about money connected to how you perceive yourself and what you are able to do, have, be?
- Describe three negative defining moments around money and how they have influenced your current attitudes and beliefs.
- Describe three positive defining moments around money and how they have influenced your current attitudes and beliefs.
- How would you describe your current relationship with money? Where do you feel empowered? Where do you feel challenged?
- What do you think it would take for you to have a healthy, empowered relationship with money? If you had your way, what would your relationship with money be even if the amount of money you have did not change?

Bonus: Create a vision for your ideal relationship with money, however you'd like to express it; draw, paint, write, use symbols or words. Take two minutes a day to spend time with this vision as a way to encourage this relationship in your life.

We Got Stats!

➡️ **Poverty rates in the U.S. vary significantly by race.** More than 20% of Native American, African-American, and Hispanic women live in poverty, compared with 9% of white women and just over 12% of Asian-American women. —Institute for Women's Policy Research (2004)

➡️ **In 2002, there were 1.3 million adult Temporary Assistance for Needy Families recipients, more than 90% of whom were women.** Over three-quarters of female TANF recipients were between 20 and 39.

—Administration for Children and Families, National TANF Date File

➡️ In 2003, there were 35.9 million people living with incomes below the federal poverty threshold. **The poverty rate for all women 18 years and older in 2003 was 12.4% (13.8 million women).** Poverty rates vary by age group among women, with the youngest women—ages 18 to 24—reporting a poverty rate of 19.7%. The lowest poverty rate (8.9%) was found among women ages 45 to 64. The poverty rate increases to 10.6% for women between 65 and 74, and to 14.3% for women 75 and older. —U.S. Census Bureau (2003)

➡️ Women in female-headed households with no spouse experience **higher rates of poverty (24.4%)** than women in married-couple families (5.2%) and men in male-headed households (8.8%).

—U.S. Census Bureau (2003)

▶

➡ Based on a 90-hour workweek, Salary.com has estimated that a **fair wage for the typical stay-at-home mom would be well over $90,000** for executing all of her daily tasks. Factor in overtime, and the appropriate salary takes a leap of around $25,000. —Salary.com

➡ Women in the United States have **no right to paid maternity,** unlike women in every other industrialized country. —America's Union Movement

Chapter 9

Wombmanifestation
Birthing Our Vision

Ain't nothing going on but the rent.

—Gwen Guthrie

Rha Rants

It's Sunday night. You're cuddled on the couch with your honey (or with your feline, your canine, or your little one) watching a little TV in an intimate moment of peace, love, and serenity. As the show winds down and the credits roll, your mind drifts toward preparation for the next morning. You're feeling one of three things: incredible excitement, because you love what you do; detached ambivalence, because it's just something that pays the bills right now; or total depression, because you have to gear up for another week of combat duty.

Take heart—all of us have been there. The wise poet and prophet Kahlil Gibran says that work should be "love made visible." But unless you have a very special arrangement with your landlord, he or she could care less about love and would rather quote *Jerry McGuire*: "Show me the money!"

We hear all the time that you can do what you love. You should do what you *love*. You can get rich doing what you love! Oh, yeah? Then how come some of the most brilliant, gifted, talented, clearly god-channeling folks I know are dirt poor? There is something missing in the equation.

Sometimes the hardest thing to do is just get clear about what you think your work is, particularly if it doesn't match already-existing occupations or preconceived notions of what a "real" job is. Add that to the hypersensitivity around others' perceptions, and there's no mystery about why most of us will just settle for something we can bear that will pay the bills.

Meanwhile, we dream of just-add-water instant success, and there are many slogans and gimmicks out there to assure us that we can have it. But very few of the "you can be rich doing what you love" messages convey the amount of focus, hard work, and support necessary to have your heart's desire.

When people ask me what I do for a living, I say that I am an artist-activist.

If I'm chilling in a poetry café, people understand exactly what that means. But when I'm traveling in my husband's world, the world of corporate lawyers, bankers, accountants, and investors, who I am and what I do becomes something that boggles even the greatest minds on Wall Street. So they smile, make passive-aggressive jokes that mask neither their ignorance nor their disdain, and change the subject.

I used to get angry. I used to want their validation. But I've come to understand that it was my own uncertainty, and need for their approval that raised these feelings.

It has taken me a long time to define my work and what I believe is my true purpose, which is to use my creative gifts to make the greatest contribution possible to the world, while still being *me*—someone with values and integrity who cares about people and the planet. I want to be someone who always has viable alternatives to selling either my ass or my soul.

It takes great passion, dedication, hard work and perseverance to go for your dreams. Achievement takes time it requires faith when you can't see it and don't know if it is ever really going to "happen," it requires a willingness to make mistake after mistake. When victory feels miles and miles away maybe even impossible, who do you become in those moments? This is an important question to ask yourself this is an important question to answer truthfully.

Work *is* love made visible, and it requires a tremendous amount of love to answer your calling; it also requires strength, courage, wisdom, faith, endurance, and a whole lot of sweat equity (that's a nice way of saying hard-ass work).

If you know what you want, that's 60 percent of the game, but what if you're just not sure?

In *The Success Book*, John Randolph Price asks: What do you believe your greatest strengths are? (Think about the things that people are always relying on you for and that may give you a clue.) What do you believe are your greatest gifts, talents? What are the things you do really well that you enjoy? Begin here. Each of us has been bestowed with strengths and gifts, and the more we ask ourselves these questions, the more the answers will begin to surface.

For some of you, the ideal job may already exist, e.g., attorney, doctor, rock star, Hollywood actress, diva socialite—these fields all require a substantial amount of focus and expertise to enter, but they are clearly attainable and there are lots of role models out there, for better or worse, who have achieved them.

But what if your calling doesn't fall into the category of a clearly defined occupation? How do you begin to create that ideal scenario? Do you have the conviction and financial wherewithal to see it through?

For those of us who have set out into unchartered waters, the most fundamental part of achieving our life's dream is to believe. How do you nurture your dreams? Do you share them with the most loving and supportive people in your life? Have you written them down? Many experts believe that you can exponentially increase the probability of achieving a goal or aspiration just by writing it down. The more *existence* you can create for your heart's desire, the more you will attract opportunities to fulfill it.

Recent statistics show that the largest demographic of new entrepreneurs is women between twenty-five and forty-five. This generation isn't settling for 76 percent of what the guys make. We are forging our own paths, so look for other women around you who could be up to the same things. Surround yourself with positive encouragement and spend time with people who love what they do.

Also, just for the record, there is no such thing as an overnight success no matter what the media tells you. So don't run in tomorrow morning and quit your job! Begin to develop a plan. Most of the people who have created their own path and achieved success doing what they loved have done so, one day at a time, one opportunity at a time.

So next Monday morning, when you go into work, celebrate and give thanks for your job if you love it. If you're just tolerating it, start to think about how you will use this opportunity as a stepping stone on the path to your ideal position. And if you're *hating*, smile even bigger, knowing that your days in this rat race are indeed numbered.

Eli Ceballos

Courageous

DJ Kuttin' Kandi

Age:
30
Cultural Identity:
Filipina
Born:
In Queens, New York
Education:
Self-graduated and
collectively educated
Occupation:
Hip-Hop DJ, producer, mentor,
teacher, writer, poet, thinker,
freedom fighter, soul survivor,
revolutionary, chant singer
Economic Class:
Failed economics senior year
Marital Status:
Married
Registered to vote:
Yes

DJ Kuttin' Kandi (aka Candice Custodio) has been a DJ for more than ten years and is a member of DJ team champions 5th Platoon, founder of and DJ for the all-female Hip-Hop group Anomolies, cofounder of the New York open mic night Guerrilla Words, and founder of the coalition R.E.A.C.Hip-Hop. Kandi has traveled all around the world performing with artists such as Bob James, Kool Herc, Jay-Z, LL Cool J, Mya, MC Lyte, Young Gunz, Dead Prez, and BlackStar. She also appears in Busta Rhymes's Much Music Special Edition video and other notable documentaries such as Scratch, *the female-DJ documentary* Mixxtress X, *and a PBS special on Filipinos in New York called* Kababayan. *She is also a spoken-word poet, a teacher and mentor of youth, and an activist and community organizer.*

❶ The poet Kahlil Gibran says, "Work is love made visible." What does this mean to you?

When you work hard for something you believe in, you are going to make sure that what you are working on shines for the entire world to see. All that hard work, all that love will shine and light so brightly that it will be visible because of all the love one will feel from it.

❷ What made you decide to be a DJ?

I wanted to be a part of the music. I didn't just want to listen to music. I wanted to be the one conducting it, playing it, and giving it out to the people. Since I wanted so much to play Hip-Hop music, being a DJ made a lot of sense.

❸ What do you believe you contribute to the world as a DJ?

A DJ has a lot of power. We have more than just the power to make people dance. We have the power to make people feel. By playing certain music, we can make people feel sad, angry, and happy. We can change the mood of a room in seconds. We also have the power to tell you what's the hottest joint and who's the illest MC out right now. We have the power to tell you what you should be into. As DJs, we have the power to control not only the airwaves and dance floors, but we have the power to control your minds. Not every DJ uses this power to contribute positively in this world. Knowing this kind of power and influence that I have as a DJ, I choose to contribute a piece of myself. I put myself out on those two turntables. I put all that I have been taught about Hip-Hop, all the positive values I've been raised with, and then I mix it with a lot of soulful love. I also know I haven't been perfect, and that I've made my mistakes along the way. I put it all out there on the tables and let it spin: "I survived." I contribute my life story, and with that I hope it helps change the world.

❹ How do you see your music and your mission being connected?

More than any other music, Hip-Hop has influenced millions and has changed the world, from the corporate giants to our young people. With that kind of power, Hip-Hop can bring both positivity and negativity. With the corporate world monopolizing Hip-Hop culture, it has been able to glorify Hip-Hop by marketing violence, sexism, and racism on radio stations, magazines, and record labels. The corporate world was able to see the kind of power and influence Hip-Hop has, and is able to bank on it. It is my mission to use Hip-Hop to speak out, express ourselves, and set ourselves free—to use it as a movement and a resistance against all that oppresses us.

❺ Why do you believe it is important to find the joy and passion in what you do for a living?

If you don't then, you're never going to get the best out of life. The best out of life comes from the people you love, the people that love you, and the things that you love doing. I believe that having a dream and being passionate about that dream fulfills a person. It's not even about whether you make it or not, it's really about giving yourself the chance and the opportunity to dream. It's about reaching the greatest potential—and the journey you take to get there—because with that travel comes great experience. That is where you find out who you are, where you come from, and where you really want to go in life, because sometimes even your original goal might not even really be what you truly wanted in the first place. It's that journey in between that will complete you. Without that journey you will find no joy or passion. Without joy or passion, you have never really lived at all.

❻ What advice would you give to struggling artists who want to just do their art, but have a hard time paying their bills?

Many people think that just because I have a "name" in the business that I am not a struggling artist. Believe me when I say this: I am a struggling artist. I am a struggling artist because I choose not to compromise my soul in a music industry that can be so cold and isolated. I make decisions to be the kind of DJ that my future children can someday be proud of and that I am proud of.

Art is a beautiful thing, especially when you love it and get to do it as a career. However, being an independent artist is still a struggle, especially when you have to deal with the reality of life. It was only four years ago that my mother, sister, and I were struggling to keep our home. When my father died of cancer, my mother was left with huge debt from medical bills. To make things worse, my mother's company of twenty years filed bankruptcy and my mother was left without a job. During that time, I was living off touring and my sister was still in college. It got to the point that we had such a hard time keeping up with the bills that our electricity would get cut off. Eventually, we lost our only home of twenty-two years, because we had to sell it before the banks foreclosed on us.

It's been a struggle for the past twelve years of my DJ career. There would be months I'd hardly ever be home, and then there would be times I wouldn't have a gig for as long as three months. The gigs ranged from your average underground open mic or a packed concert of 15,000. Either way, I was always hustling. Whenever I noticed that I only had a few gigs in a year, I'd go back to a full-time or part-time job. I'd work at corporate marketing companies as a billing clerk, financial assistant, or administrative assistant. During hard times there really aren't many choices but to work the jobs you'd hate to do. Of course, I would never recommend sellin' out or sellin' your soul. But if you're in the life of the hustle, which is like the music business, you do what you've got to do to survive. Always have a backup job, always have something lined up, and always be prepared for the days you don't have a gig or a tour. Being a DJ is like the perfect avenue. We work at night so we always have the opportunity to work a good job during the daytime and then by night we're out spinning for the nightlife. A lot of other artists have the same opportunity. It's just part of being a struggling artist. Oh yeah, be prepared to hardly have any sleep!

❼ What do you love about the work you do?

I love the fact that I can wake up each morning knowing that I am going to do a job that I don't regret doing. I love the fact that I can go to work knowing that the first thing I see are young faces full of energy, full of life, and full of hope. I love the fact that I get to pass down knowledge to other people. Working for young people gives me the opportunity to help create a change in the world because young people are part of that change. Out of all the accomplishments

I've ever had, mentoring these young people is probably the greatest one.

❽ How long did it take for you to get into your ideal job?

My life story has been a journey for me. It's such a long journey that I am still traveling on it. I don't even label my DJ career a "job." It's just part of my journey, taking me somewhere in my life to teach me something. So because this journey is so long, I really feel no time frame and I really don't consider anything an "ideal job." It's a moment in time for me, teaching me something about my purpose in my life. It's also a moment in time for me to give something of myself to others.

❾ What characteristics did you personally need in order to succeed in your work domain?

To be able to succeed in the music industry you need to be all about hustlin' and putting your game face on. You need to be proactive and you need to be ready, willing, and able. I'm great at everything else but "ready, willing, and able." I'm not down to do anything and everything just to "make it" in this business. I have my beliefs and I won't compromise. The music business is known for compromising artists' beliefs and standards. So, if you're a person like me who will not conform, who has morals and values other than to survive in this game, then you should hustle even more. With your political beliefs, it will be much harder for you to land gigs. Promoters, record labels, and others won't always be so open to hiring you if you're going to say something or do something that they don't want to be attached to, which is why you should always know who you want to work with so you don't have to come across these people. You also need a lot of patience, because there will be times and days it won't be easy. You also need to be honest with yourself as much as possible. When you're working in the music world, it can get so loud sometimes that you forget to listen to yourself and your true instincts.

❿ How do you avoid burnout?

There are times I work too hard that I forget to take time out for myself. I always feel committed to everyone and everything, because I am committed to everyone and everything. I never want to say no, because I always want to be a part of every cause, goal, and mission that touches my heart. This is why we need to take time out to listen to ourselves. Our body and our mind speaks to us, and it tells us when we're about to shut down. It tells us when we're tired and it tells us when our spirits are down. I'm such a strong believer in taking care of self and doing for self first before anyone else. In this activist world, it is so important to remember that the revolution starts within, and I can't be no revolutionary if I don't exist. I need to be around to continue this important work so I need to take time out for me.

How do I take care of me? As stubborn as I am, I fight my need of wanting to be a part of everything and I take time out. I take short day vacations for myself and do things that relax me. I paint, I practice my guitar, I read a book, I write poetry. Or I'll just spend time with my *mahal*, Rob.

Also, part of taking care of you is being able to enjoy your time with people you love to be with. Sometimes, I get so caught up with just being around people in the music business or people in the movement that I forget there are other people who I love in my life who are not part of either. Part of me feeling good is spending time with them and having fun.

⓫ How do you incorporate activism into your work?

Hip-Hop itself is political. It was born during political times for political reasons. The history of Hip-Hop exemplifies what people will do when they are oppressed, for with oppression comes great expression. Hip-Hop is probably one of the greatest resources we have to use to make change in this world and to fight for social justice.

So, I bring all of this knowledge of Hip-Hop into all that I do, whether I'm speaking at panels, workshops, teach-ins, or classes I teach.

Also, the Hip-Hop name that I made for myself in this business carries so much power and responsibility. I choose to be proactive and speak about the work that needs to be done within all of our communities.

⓬ What are the elements of a successful career?

People always ask me what's next for me. What's the next gig? What's the next move for you to make it, Kandi? For me, I've already "made it." I'm pretty content in my life because I feel very accomplished. To some, "making it" is being on some radio show or putting out a record and making the millions. Through all that I've experienced in my life, I have learned to be content with what I've got. First, I've survived through some really hard times in my life. My family and I survived my father's death, losing our home, losing a job, losing electricity, and going into debt. I have survived losing friendships and losing a love relationship. I have survived a friend's death, I have survived almost losing my own self. I have survived my own self-oppression. I survived some pretty bad youthful years that could have taken me to prison or homelessness or death. To survive all of that is a big success for me.

People define success differently, but for me success is being able to survive the bad times and to make the most out of every situation. Success is seeing the good out of every worst possible scenario. Success is being able to turn something negative into something positive. My success isn't defined by anything material, but in the fact that I can wake up every day feeling good that I didn't sell my soul. It's the fact that I look at the young people I work with and know that I am one of the reasons why they're going to be successful, too. It's the fact that I feel good when I hear someone tell me that I've inspired them, and changed their life.

Of course, I always have something next to do, because I'm a big believer in making a dream come true. It's an even greater feeling when I know I don't have to compromise myself or anyone else in order to fulfill that dream.

Stranger I-Land

by Ariana Green

I am a journalist 'cause there are infinite stories to tell. I write so the people here know of the people there. So here and there lose meaning. I write 'cause I don't *entender*, not enough.

"Filiberto Ojeda Ríos Killed by FBI"—this happened in Puerto Rico when I was there for fifteen months, self-chosen displacement in search of a journalistic life's education.

I covered Filiberto's death for a major U.S. newspaper. The compatriots who served seventeen years behind bars for a crime committed with Ojeda Ríos spoke to me as if I were their daughter: "*Mi hija*, times have changed, violence is not the answer. Filiberto had already learned, but the United States, the assassins, wanted to make a statement on our day."

Problem: I was not *la hija*. I was outside looking in.

Yet I and they were one—living, sharing, breathing island gusts that bring the cancer rate down by cleaning up carcinogens, while enabling pollution of a more poignant sort to permeate streets with beggars blocking weaving cars.

Journalism, in its many forms, is humbling; I can never know enough, be sufficiently immersed in what I observe or attempt to assess. Any foreign correspondent new to a place fights to grasp what others comprehend without trying. Tough, yes, but with rewards aplenty: I speak intimately with people I do not know, I use the power of the press to reveal fresh narratives. I seek to earn trust. Answers, however nebulous, emerge in installments.

"American Supermarket Chains Beat Out Local Farmers"

It's my work to find the story: rotting, globalized, *cambiando*. Get it right, report it like it is.

On the island, it didn't much matter that I was Jewish, that my grandparents grew up in Iraq, that I had an Ivy League education. What mattered was that I could listen and talk back. What mattered was my attempt to dole out semblances of poetic justice, to confront a truth that is elusive, to track for a place that is ours.

Ariana Green is a twenty-three-year-old Iraqi-Jewish-American journalist from Cambridge, Massachusetts, now living in New York City. She works at NBC News and has written for the New York Times, San Juan *magazine,* Popular Science, *and other publications. A graduate of Brown University, she spent fifteen formative months in Puerto Rico after school.*

Meditations of a Wiggle-Wart (WhiteGirl Activist Serenity Prayer)

by Chelsea Michel Gregory

When I was a little girl, my grandpa would always call me "wiggle-wart" because I could never stop moving. To this day I am in constant motion, drawn to people and places that enable me to be the artist-activist-advocate-educator shoulder-to-cry-on sure-you-can-stay-for-a-while-hon I'll-fix-you-a-plate-if-you-want-some-and-take-these-vitamins-if-you're-sick girl-don't-you-even-stress-it-here's-what-we're-gonna-do-big-sister-baby-sitter-long-distance-makeshift-family-com-munity-builder woman that I aspire to be . . .

. . . but what if I just had to be me?
what if I had to set my own priorities?
what if I had to let go of all these things
I have worked so long and hard to prove?

In my dreams I move with confidence in directions that have yet to
    be mapped
I let my motivation be the intention that is the impulse of my heart
    strapped
with the gat of goodwill 'cause willingness is the weapon that will
enable me to make these moves
and stillness is the sanctuary in which dream becomes truth.

Chelsea Michel Gregory *is a white, Jewish, Brooklyn-based artist, activist, and educator originally from Atlanta, Georgia.*

rant

my work is ecstasy

by Fly Yvonne O. Etaghene

cashier, dishwasher, event planner, magazine editor, teaching artist, queen of temp agencies, freelance writer, personal chef, grassroots organizer, tutor, cleaning lady, phone-sex operator, telemarketer, playwright, workshop facilitator, panel member, gas station attendant, shoe store saleswoman, librarian's assistant, knife saleswoman, my own tour manager and booking agent, student, poet, daughter, woman, et cetera.

in one of my poems I write:
"I don't want to know whether
you liked my rhyming skills (but)
did I connect with your soul?"

the purpose of my art has always been to find ways to make my poetry functional so you walk away with more than just another memory of another dope show you went to, but with words that describe your pain and joy and that equip you with a few more tools for your continued physical and spiritual survival in this beautiful and fucked-up world. I want mine to be the poetry that keeps you living, loving and challenging. as black dykes, *we are on the periphery of the margin of the fringes* and I use this art not necessarily to access the mainstream space we are continually denied entry into, but to create entirely new space(s) for us.

my love for poetry is the passion in my pocket driving me to spit verses from brooklyn to detroit to oakland. I organized one-woman shows and two national tours for the love; I shared my heart through my words in parks and across kitchen tables for the love; and now I feel like taking a break from performing! who am I if I'm not on stage? and, of course: what next?

it's not so much what next, as *what always?* I will always be a poet, on or off stage, I will always be a dancer, whether with my feet, fingertips, or the verses that spill from me; I will always be creative, whether by crocheting the brightest of colors together and wrapping my body in the stitches I lovingly made or cooking savory, sweet melodies in curry-mango flavored pots and sharing my tasty, edible songs with friends, family, and strangers.

I choose to do what only makes my spirit sing and I trust in the universe to provide me with financial abundance. *don't get it twisted*—I do work my ass off! I also deeply love what I do because what I do is a reflection of who I be—never the other way around.

Fly Yvonne O. Etaghene *is a twenty-five-year-old Nigerian woman-loving-woman poet raised in Ithaca, New York.*

Calling All Leaders—Where the Ladies At?

by Yvonne Bynoe

Where does a young woman go to learn how to become a leader? Let me rephrase that: Where does a young working-class woman go, or a young woman of color go, or a young women who lacks a four-year college degree go, or a young mother go to learn how to lead? Women have made advances in the corporate and public sectors, yet the pool of young women who enter the leadership pipeline remains small and homogenous. Studies have shown that the young women who become bona fide leaders are disproportionately white, full-time college students who have parents who are engaged in civic and political activities. Unfortunately, many non–college women are not involved in their communities and as a result do not gain leadership experience. Moreover, many young women, because of their race, socioeconomic background, or marital status are not encouraged to believe that they have voices that matter in society. Developing a cadre of female leaders, whose pedigrees are indistinguishable from their male counterparts, will not necessarily promote the interests of all women. Our democracy needs diverse perspectives included in the public dialogue. How then do we get more and different types of young women on the leadership path?

Young women of color, young working-class women, young non–college women, and young mothers need mentors who can provide advice and guidance; they need hands-on experience and they need role models, people like themselves who have overcome obstacles to become leaders. A leader organizes people and empowers them to translate a vision into reality. Given this definition, there are older women in virtually every neighborhood in the country who can serve as leadership mentors and role models to young women. The activism of several women influenced me to use my writing as a vehicle for political and social change. I now write books and articles and speak publicly with the hope that my work and accomplishments will spur young women to action, into leadership.

The key to getting more young women to see themselves as leaders is get them to see the women around them as leaders. We have to convince young women of color, young working-class women, young non–college women, and young mothers that the woman who organizes the annual block party is a leader, as is the woman who is active in her church. Similarly, the woman who organizes her neighbors to get a traffic light placed in a dangerous intersection is an activist, just like the mother who leads a fundraising campaign to buy computers for her child's school. Leadership is not a birthright, it is the prerogative of anyone bold enough to endeavor to alter the status quo.

Yvonne Bynoe *is the author of* Stand & Deliver: Political Activism, Leadership and Hip Hop Culture *(Soft Skull Press) and* The Encyclopedia of Rap and Hip Hop Culture *(Greenwood Press). She is also a regular contributor to the National Public Radio program* News & Notes *with Ed Gordon.*

Keep sowing the seeds that give life, keep manifesting the words spoken in your rhymes, keep creating the design of your life, take action, keep those promises coming, revolution through your action.
—Lea Monique Chavez, "My Wild Love"

I Don't Love My Job, But I Do Love Money

by Desiree Chinnery

Ultimately, I want to be in the career of marketing or new product development, but right now, I'm in corporate America, working it and working it well.

My philosophy on work is to be the best at whatever I am doing. Anyone can be taught to do anything, and with the proper training we can all be great. I was always the one who did all of her homework growing up, because I liked looking good and having the answers. I never wanted to be embarrassed by being unprepared, and that is the work ethic I still carry today. I work very hard and I am known as the go-to person. I'm like Toni Childs on *Girlfriends*; I specialize in results. I currently work at a large corporation in the investment bank training area. I like what I do, but it doesn't drive me. I'm driven by the comfortable lifestyle that I've built for myself, and the comfortable bank account that I'm also building. There is nothing for me here spiritually. This is a job, not a career. This is a large corporation with over 160,000 employees, and I'm recognized in my area of risk management and I am being groomed to do great things. I am being invested in and I am a top performer.

This is all great, but it doesn't light me up. It feels good to know that my work ethic has allowed me to succeed at everything I do, even if it's not what I'm passionate about. There are also benefits to working for a large corporation, such as work and personal life balance. My company is a great place to work for if you are a minority. I don't have any children now, but if I did there are flexible work schedules and day care facilities for me to utilize. My benefits are awesome. But this is how they get you. They give you just enough to get really comfortable in your life so when you look at leaving to do something meaningful or that you are passionate about, you don't do it cause you don't want to lose the nice cushion that you have created for yourself. You don't want to start over, and you keep telling yourself, "Next year I will go back to school, next year I will start my own business, next year I will do this and that," and you know what? Next year never comes. This is the boat I am in and before you know it, if I don't make a different choice, I will be thirty years old and still working a job and not establishing a career.

Desiree Chinnery *is a twenty-five-year old successful, outgoing woman from New York City. She can be found honoring spirit and giving love.*

Black women have to work hard every day to keep their jobs, pay their rent, look decent, and keep food on the table. I think it is important to sacrifice in other ways for your children. And, for me, this means sometimes putting work and career on the back burner. —Zenzele Isoke, Hip-Hop activist

Life Is Not a Career

by Nichim

At twenty-seven, I choose to become a mother. My partner had arrived like a nymph three months earlier, my mother died six months after, and I found myself with child and partner broke, back in my country three months after my daughter's birth. It's been quite a journey. Now, back in Brooklyn, after letting go of trying to control my life, I find myself thinking, "Life is perfect." I've learned that when you trust, you are led to where you need to be. I had a career and was learning to climb the ladder. But sure enough, the moment I said, "I trust," I met my partner and we got pregnant. Since then, I've learned that I control very little in my life, but I trust that I am where I need to be. That is my work.

My career has shifted from being a youth educator to educating our child and myself about being self sufficient human beings. From beginning to end our day is filled with awesome moments that will be lingering memories to retell. Primarily, though, our days are free. We get to choose the way we want to spend them. We go on daily adventures. We get to learn how to mop, climb trees, walk on wet earth, fly down the slide at the playground, dance to Olantunji, sing "Itsy Bitsy Spider," real loud on the train, learn to play with friends, make art, stay in our pajamas all day, and be beautiful.

I get to live life each day as I choose to. I get to dream and rediscover myself not only as a mother but as a woman. I get to be the singer, the dancer, the artist, the inventor, the scientist, the educator, the organizer, the botanist, the herbalist, the amazing cook. I get to relax on the couch after a long day of motherhood and simmer on how awesome my life is.

I know that it won't always be like this, that social pressure won't always allow me to be a mother and have fun doing it. Motherhood has taught me that I can make choices, and we figure out creative ways to support ourselves as mothers so that we can be mothers. We can work with our partners to create stable homes, so that responsibilities are shared and we can both be selves, lovers, artists, and parents at the same time.

While becoming a mother can be scary, it doesn't have to be. It can be an ocean of awesome opportunities; it can be a time to raise ourselves while we raise our children. It can be a time to imagine and play, to have fun with life, to laugh every day. It can be a time to bring community together for the support and upbringing of our children. Mothering is not an isolating experience. It is a communal experience that requires us to let go of our hang-ups about being young mothers in a modern world and open ourselves up to receive the gifts our children bring to us.

It's a time for women to come together and share resources, maternity clothes, baby clothes, birth stories, or just a shoulder to rest on when a mama needs it. We don't need to be rich with money from an amazing career to be mothers; we need to be open to give and receive, to ask for what we need, and to do what is needed. Money, time, and even open doors begin to show up like magic when one learns to trust. It's a risk well worth taking. After working nonstop for half of my life, taking this time to focus on becoming a mother is well worth the times we've struggled with nine dollars in the bank, the fear and doubt, the having to ask for help, the moving in with your parents for some time.

I love what I do, and I am so in love with my family, grateful for having the chance to grow into myself a little bit more each day, for experiencing what it means to mother, for having the chance to dream and realize all my visions. I just want to let you know that it is possible! Ask for what you need, and watch it come to you.

And to many of us who love our careers, we'll find the break to be a needed breath that will shed light into our next steps as amazing women.

Nichim *resides in Brooklyn but claims the world as her ground for learning. Along with her delicious partner and superwarrior daughter, she is in the process of making a move to a secret location to learn how to install solar panels, purify water, and start an organic farm.*

What's Work Got to Do with It?
Taking the Long View on Work, Making a Difference, and Happiness

by Anna Lappé

The future is shaped in the present. What is important is not the fulfillment of all one's dreams, but the stubborn determination to continue dreaming. We will have grandchildren, and they will have children too. The world will continue, and whether we know it or not, we are deciding its course every day.
> —Gioconda Belli, author and former Nicaraguan Sandinista

On my desk are a batch of bills that need tending, a to-do list with line items that if they were milk would long since be curdled, and a message light on my phone blinking like a nagging kid. Outside my window, the streets are peopled again; it's Sunday, and nearly summer. But I have work to do, so I glue myself to my seat to get through some of those bills, to-dos, and to write this—to say something about "work," the choices we make about how we spend our days, and, of course, how we put roofs over our heads.

Just above my computer is a postcard a friend sent from Miami of Frida Kahlo. She leans back in a wooden-armed chair, her self-portrait just above her head; a cigarette dangles from her left hand. She looks at the camera as if making a dare. When I get stuck or frustrated with my work, I meet her gaze. What's her dare? I have no idea, so I made one up: I dare you to work hard, to wrap your hands around each day, to become a part of a lineage of those who've come before you—and will come after you—trying to make this world better.

Make the world better? Some dare. Yes, I know, it often feels like an impossible task. OK, it *always* feels like an impossible task. When we hear daily news like today's headlines: The Kentucky Derby gets top billing, but beneath it, news from a crumbling CIA, a worsening Iraq, a deteriorating Afghanistan; more bad news. In a world where genocides flare, where 20,000 children die every day from preventable disease, where Anchorage, Alaska becoming a beach resort seems like a serious possibility, it certainly does feel impossible.

So how can our work make any dent at all? That question is answered for me by these words from Salvadoran archbishop Oscar Romero, who was an outspoken critic of human rights abuses in his country until his assassination during a mass in 1980. Despite his murder, his words and life's work inspired a generation of human rights advocates in that country, and beyond. Romero said:

> It helps now and then, to step back and take the long view. The kingdom is not only beyond our efforts, it is even beyond our vision . . . Nothing we do is complete, which is another way of saying that the kingdom always lies beyond us. No statement captures all that should be said. No prayer fully expresses our faith. No confession brings perfection. No set of goals and objectives includes everything. We plant the seeds that one day will grow. We water seeds already planted, knowing they hold future promise. We cannot do everything and there is a sense of liberation in that. This enables us to do something and do it very well. It may be incomplete, but it is the beginning.

Everything is connected, that the seemingly disparate crises of racism, poverty and hunger, environmental degradation, and violence against women are all interrelated. If we understand their common roots and current connections, then we can get that whatever we choose to work on can play a role in addressing the roots of all these crises.

It's Sunday, and I have to finish this piece and I have work to do, yes. I have a pile of papers I'm supposed to read and a few new reports: one, about strategies to shift billions of taxpayer dollars away from big business and toward small farmers and the hungry; another, about how Monsanto, the world's largest biotech company, has just bought the world's largest seed repository, giving it control of a greater and greater share of our food supply. But that's not the real reason I have to stop writing. A friend is swinging by any minute, and I'll jump on my bike to head down to a warehouse on Flatbush. We have a party to go to.

Anna Lappé is an author, public speaker, and advocate for the radical idea that "grub"—local, healthy, sustainable food—should be available to all of us. She currently lives in Brooklyn, where she appreciates the six-second commute to her office.

This is our one shot to make a difference and no one is going to make it for us.
—Jacqueline Rappoport, graduate student

Tribe

by Adeeba Rana

Sisters, create!
Create and revel in the glory of handcrafted, crystalline wisdom.
Tiny slivers of sun, dropped one by one into crevices and cracks,
creating an eye-popping mural.
Craft, and watch what becomes.
A new tree of life, laden with fruit.
The fruit of one's labor is always rich,
but better still is the lingering aftertaste of sweet sugarcane sisterhood.
Create, and nurture, and heal.
Remember, the days of creation are not over,
and you do not travel alone.

Adeeba Rana is an eighteen-year-old Pakistani-American poet and student who resides in Massachusetts.

Ritual of Empowerment

Ideal Work Vision

What is your vision of the contribution you want to make to the world? How can you deepen and strengthen the context for your work so that it becomes more about what you want to see in the world and less about the next gig or job? What are you really passionate about?

The following questions come from Gail Straub and David Gershon's book *Empowerment: The Art of Creating Your Life as You Want It (High Point Press, 1989)* (www.empowermenttraining.org), and are designed to help you develop your ideal work vision. This ritual normally takes thirty to forty-five minutes.

Find a quiet place where you won't be disturbed. Give yourself the time and space to explore the following questions in whatever form works best for you (writing, drawing, collage, and so on). Materials you might want are magazines, glue sticks, markers, glitter, crayons, and construction paper.

In your ideal vision of work:

- What are the values that drive your work vision? Be as specific as you can. (love, joy, peace, adventure, and so on . . .)

- Which of your talents, gifts, and/or skill sets are you currently using? What are the challenges you have that allow you to grow, stretch, and fully express your unique gifts?
- How do you structure your work? Are you working solo or with others? Are you managing others? Are you traveling? How many hours a day and days of the week do you work? How is your current structure working for or against your work vision?
- Describe the kind of people you are working with, and the kind of relationships that support your work moving forward. Describe the quality of communication with these people. Describe the effect your presence has on the people you work with.

When your answers feel complete, create a practice of spending time with this vision for five minutes before you start your work day. Notice what's already in place; be sure to affirm and celebrate these things. Brainstorm ideas for how you will achieve and incorporate the other elements of your vision.

We Got Stats!

➡️ **One third of female board members of Fortune 1000 companies graduated from women's colleges.**
—Nikki V. Katz. About.com

➡️ 20% of the women identified by *Black Enterprise* magazine as the 20 **most powerful African-American women in corporate America graduated from women's colleges.**
—Nikki V. Katz. About.com

➡️ **61% of firms owned by women of color are in the service sector**; 12.4% are in retail trade; and 4.0% are in goods-producing industries including construction, mining, manufacturing, and agriculture. —Center for Women's Research (2004)

➡️ As of 2004, there are an estimated **1.4 million privately held firms owned by women of color in the U.S.**, employing nearly 1.3 million people and generating nearly $147 billion in sales.
—Center for Women's Research (2004)

➡️ **The pay gap between men and women remained relatively unchanged from 1983 to 2000. Women on average were paid 44% less than men.** —America's Union Movement. (2003)

➡️ **Overall, labor force participation rates will continue to rise** among women and edge down among men between 1998 and 2008. —U.S. Department of Labor (2000)

➡ In 2003, **3.7 million women had multiple jobs.**
—The Business and Professional Women's Foundation

➡ 72% of part-time workers are women and **more than one million women earn wages below the federal minimum wage.**
—The Business and Professional Women's Foundation

➡ From 1997 to 2004, the greatest **growth in the number of women-owned firms** was in construction, transportation/communications, and agricultural services.
—The Business and Professional Women's Foundation

➡ 1 in every 11 adult women in the U.S. owns a business. **Female entrepreneurship has been growing** at twice the national average since 1997.
—The Business and Professional Women's Foundation

Chapter 10

Who's World Is This?
Mine. Yours. Ours.

Why is the system torturing you? You pay taxes, you wear blue jeans, you eat burgers.

—Lenelle Moïse, "Cruel and Unusual Punishment,"
from the We Got Issues! Performance Piece

Rha Rants

Damn right! We are as (hyphen-dash-hyphen) American as they come. We eighteen-to-thirty-five-year-olds are 30 million strong in this country alone, but only 35 percent of us felt inspired enough to get our blue jeans to the polls in the last presidential election. But before we go there, let's break down citizenship as we see it!

Back in the day, when our illustrious founding fathers dipped their feathers to ink the Bill of Rights, they had no idea what they were getting themselves into. More than two centuries later, the dream of a true democracy continues to elude us, serving as a more of a shimmering mirage than a tangible reality.

I am a change-of-life baby, born in the late '60s to parents who were born in the late '20s. That means my Hip-Hop is heavily imbued with the struggle for civil rights. My parents endured the journey from nigga to colored to negro to black to African American right on back to nigga again—and they made sure that my siblings and I knew the value of an education and the importance of being able to give back. What it also meant is that we were infused with the psychology of limitation—because "whitey," as he was so affectionately called, "will never let you have anything."

So we worked twice as hard, cleaned up twice as good, studied even longer, and became masterful at how to smile and put "the man" at ease. We understood that our safety and our ability to make a living depended on it.

My parents were extremely politically active. My father worked as an attorney with the local NAACP chapter while trying criminal cases for Legal Aid at twelve dollars a day; he knew Malcolm and Martin. My equally ambitious mother worked with the Urban League, Operation Push, and, finally, the Rainbow Coalition; she even ran for office, becoming a district party leader in our community. Long before we knew what political organizing meant, my siblings and I were getting signatures on ballot petitions; stuffing, licking, and mailing thousands of envelopes; palm carding; poll watching; and most important, registering hundreds and hundreds of people to vote.

Bookended by the long hours put in by my dedicated parents, we had a very clear and inspiring context for political involvement, and our efforts felt real—we were supporting good people who cared about our community.

Sir Webster defines a citizen as "a member of a state or nation, especially one with a republican form of government, who gives allegiance to it by birth or naturalization and is entitled to full civil rights."

We, however, would like to offer a different spin:

WGI! sees American citizenship as the cultivation of a national *relationship* based on the promise, vision, and ideals of equality, justice, and freedom for all—also known as life, liberty, and the pursuit of happiness.

Based on this definition, how are we and the United States doing?

In 1984, I was heavily involved in Jesse Jackson's presidential campaign. The excitement was tangible, and it was all the black folks in our community would talk about. Though Jesse didn't win the nomination, we knew the name of the game was to rally enough support to ensure that he would continue to be a major player in the party, who could negotiate on behalf of our people. When he gave his speech at the '84 Democratic convention his voice rang true, loud, and clear; I felt proud, connected, and successful. And his message wasn't just about black people, it was about all of us.

Somewhere between 1984 and 1988, Jesse's message shifted. The conviction seemed to soften, the intention felt muddled, and platitudes became the order of the day. Jesse seemed very concerned about pissing people off. When he ran again in 1988, I was less enthused; by that time the antiapartheid movement and Tawana Brawley had consumed most of my attention. One day while in a restaurant, I overheard a discussion, "You know what Jesse's problem is? He actually believes that he can win." That misperception alone was enough to have black folks render him out of touch.

What began as a movement to provide inspiration and access to many of the poor and marginalized people of this nation had became about a personal agenda for ambition, and the thousands of hours I had worked to support this vision felt wasted. At the ripe old age of twenty-one, I was done with politics. I continued to vote, because any black person who understands the struggle for this right and the legacy of blood that surrounds it feels obligated to go to the polls—and I was no exception.

But my belief in politics, my belief in our ability to impact larger government, my belief that at the end of the day, when all the babies had been kissed that any of these well-dressed, polished, articulate, talking heads who expressed "genuine" concern about the plight of the poor and disenfranchised would even remember any of us a hundred days after their election into office was dead and stinking.

In its first phase, We Got Issues! spent thirteen months traveling the country and coming face-to-face with almost 1,000 young women. And after sitting with the hearts, minds, and concerns of our sisters, here's what we found out:

- Young women want and need encouragement to raise our voices in an authentic way about politics.
- Young women's empowerment is directly proportional to our ability to create a healthy tribe and community.
- Many young women, particularly women of color, fear power, yet they

hold great aspirations for themselves and their communities.

So how does this generation begin to recognize that even though our citizenship may not take the form of waving from bannered platforms or kissing babies for the benefit of the camera, we do matter, and what we provide for this country *counts?*

The redefinition of our citizenship lies less in what we ultimately decide to do and more in how much we are willing to honor and acknowledge our contributions.

Our everyday nurturing, nourishing, and caring for our respective communities is just as vital and significant as running a multimillion dollar corporation or leading a nationwide demonstration for civil rights.

And while on the topic of civil rights . . . how does our decision to vote or not to vote impact the issues we care most about?

Our citizenship cannot be defined through one simple act; it must be seen as an accumulation of ongoing acts that are consistent with a partnership rooted in achieving the promise, vision, and ideals of a true democracy.

On November 5, 2001, I made a conscious decision to redefine my relationship with America; I had inherited a relationship from my parents and ancestors, but I felt it was time to create my own. I felt that I could no longer afford to see myself as this disenfranchised, disadvantaged, at-risk minority who needed "massa's" approval to be counted. I could no longer bash this nation without acknowledging all of the incredible things it has afforded me, and I could no longer pretend that I was not responsible for the perpetuation of everything I despised—even if that responsibility came through my own inaction.

If I am responsible, what am I willing and able to do to create the kind of community, society, and nation I envision?

Ladies, it's time to *step up!*

We must begin to stand in our own power, carrying both the privilege and responsibility required to take this nation closer to its dreams.

We must be willing to see ourselves as part of the big picture, offering support and accountability where it is needed.

And most importantly we must be willing to reclaim our status, as this nation's better half (no offense, guys) and start handling our business

After all, we pay taxes, we eat burgers, we wear blue jeans . . .

Empowered

Wanda Vazquez-Firpi

Originally from San Sebastián, Puerto Rico, Wanda Vázquez-Firpi grew up in the Brownsville section of Brooklyn. She is the first in her family to graduate from college, and holds degrees in psychology and education from York College and Brooklyn College. Wanda is an assistant principal at El Puente Academy for Peace and Justice in Brooklyn. She also facilitates junior English and the women's group, and is the cocoordinator of the academy's annual Hip-Hop Showcase and Woman's Day Celebration. Both of these events are coproduced with the young people of the academy.

Age:

30

Cultural Identity:

Puerto Rican

Born:

In Puerto Rico

Education:

Masters

Occupation:

Educator

Economic Class:

Middle class

Marital Status:

Married

Registered to Vote:

Yes

❶ Do you consider yourself a U.S. citizen? In what ways?

I was born in Mayaguez, Puerto Rico. By virtue of the fact that Borinquen remains a colony of the United States, I am therefore a citizen of the United States. Regardless of whether or not I consider myself a U.S. citizen, my birth certificate deems me so. Politics aside, this is an important fact, since it means that I have access to certain material resources to which those who lack U.S. citizenship do not. I certainly feel a great affinity to my Puerto Rican heritage and, although being a U.S. citizen from Puerto Rico may very well amount to a form of second-class citizenship, people risk their lives to get into this country. I, on the other hand, can come and go as I please.

This of course is a highly complicated issue, especially when you begin to consider how gender intersects with citizenship, ethnicity, and participation in civic life. At any rate, I'm not so sure how much it matters whether I consider myself a citizen of this nation or not. I do know that to deny my citizenship would also be to deny a degree of undeniable privilege, despite the racism, discrimination, and contradictions I have to face.

❷ How would you describe your relationship to this country?

When I was a child, my father worked at a factory during the week and sold *pinchos* (shish kabobs) and *piraguas* (snow cones) on the weekends to make ends meet. My mother was a full-time homemaker who labored overtime each day taking care of all of us. My mother has always been as she is now: beautiful and strong. As a woman, she has had to endure many hardships in life.

In 1980 we moved to Brooklyn, where Spanish was rarely spoken outside of the two-bedroom apartment in which we lived. Spanish was not spoken at the stores on "Pingking" (Pitkin) Avenue, the health clinic, the welfare office, or school. Like many who try to keep moving every day just to get by, getting out of the ghetto was not within the realm of possibility for us. Having to navigate the system took a lot of hard work. We endured an enormous amount of hurt and pain as U.S. citizens living in poverty. For example, I often had to miss school in order to translate on behalf of my family members whenever they needed to see a doctor or if they had a face-to-face interview appointment at "Guilfredo's" (the welfare and public assistance office). It was awful. The social workers were always so rude to us, maybe because whichever family member I accompanied spoke not a word of English. Or maybe they were just overworked and underpaid. Either way, being treated in such a fashion infuriated me.

Fortunately, I have been able to transform these feelings of anger, hostility, and rage into something positive. These negative experiences, in other words, were formative. They animate so many of my commitments and desires—to always have a voice, to overcome obstacles, to treat people like the human beings that they are. I guess there's a certain love/hate quality to my relationship with and history within this country.

❸ How did you come to this particular form of activism? How is it related to your citizenship and the citizenship of others?

I went to school in one of the worst districts in Brooklyn, an area where cops and newscasters were often present covering one unfortunate event after another. They would quickly jump out of the car, cover their story, and run back in and out of the "'hood." As a student, I was in the gifted program, the main benefit of which was the extra attention teachers gave me. Looking back, one teacher in particular stands out—Ms. Enoch, who taught English. She's the person who originally sparked my interest in literature, an interest that has remained very much alive in me ever since.

My work at El Puente Academy for Peace and Justice has allowed me to inspire others through education. I may not be an activist in the traditional sense, but I am very much involved in a day-to-day struggle to build a sense of community within the school, particularly amongst the students. They face many of the same challenges that I faced as a young woman of color.

❹ Do you see yourself as a leader?

Whenever I speak in front of the young women I work with at the academy, there's a certain look in their eyes. It's a kind of mirror that does indeed lead me to see myself as a leader. These young women have learned so much in the short amount of time that we've been working together. The questions they ask indicate that they have reached a heightened sense of awareness—about social injustice, violence against women, the benefits of eating healthily.

❺ What continues to inspire you to live and work in this country?

Young people. In particular, the young women I work with each day. When I was their age, I was desperate for a safe place to go to, for a space where I'd feel loved and appreciated, where my opinion would matter. Somewhere I could ask questions, where I might receive guidance on how to survive as a woman of color in this racist, sexist society we live in. When I wasn't busy cultivating my self-hatred as a young woman in the ghetto, I was desperately looking for a way out. I feel that I am able to provide this safe, nurturing space for the young women at El Puente. Witnessing them develop and progress inspires me every day.

❻ How are young women conditioned to participate (or not) in the governing of this country? Why is it important for America's daughters to contribute?

Our society has taught women to not question things, to simply accept the status quo and not make a fuss about everything that's wrong with this world. From childhood we are basically taught that a woman must "know her place." Well, I've stood in that place, and I decided long ago never to stand there again. I know my place. It's to question the world, and to act on such questioning. My place is to raise my voice when I need to. My place is to never stop asking questions of others and myself. It is to have self-determination.

Tuesday

by Adeeba Rana

Yesterday,
I went to vote.
The place was rife with purpose,
committed political values and headstrong ideals.

Yesterday, I caught up with a friend.
She told me about the first blow job she ever gave,
I told her this was my first vote.
The reactions were the same;
She got, "That was good baby,"
words that made her feel hollow inside.
I didn't even get words.
The TV screen
blinked devil red,
with only splotches of healing blue.

It seems some experiences
are ungratifying.
Blow jobs and elections
leave hollow boxes
where intimate words should be.

Adeeba Rana *is an eighteen-year-old Pakistani-American poet and student who resides in Massachusetts.*

Once Upon a Time in Puerto Rico

by Raquel Z. Rivera

Once upon a time, when I was still living in Puerto Rico, I did take part in a political campaign. It was the early '90s, for the plebiscite where voters could choose between three options: statehood, commonwealth, or independence. I joined the campaign for what became known as the Fourth Option: not participating in the electoral circus at all. The whole idea of the plebiscite was ridiculous: nothing but a beauty contest and a big waste of money. The outcome of the vote meant nothing; it was nonbinding, meaning that the U.S. Congress would have to do nothing about it, just "listen" to the will of the people. Stupid! So I chose to make a statement by loudly announcing, through marches and caravans along with thousands of others, that I would not be voting.

Electoral politics is not the only pathway to productive social change. Its one of the pathways—and one for which I have very little patience. I have much respect for those people with a conscience who choose electoral politics as their method to bring about change. But community organizing, education, cultural activism, and self-discovery are just as important. And that's where I've chosen to participate most actively—until the next issue or candidate comes around that really moves me to go to the voting booth.

But lately I have been wondering, maybe I can go further if I forsake this strategy of being a registered voter who hardly ever votes. Maybe I should regularly participate in all the elections, even if I don't care for any of the options. Maybe I should do a blank vote or a write-in vote (Zora Neale Hurston, Jesus Christ, Mother Jones, my mom . . .) But do those votes even count? Or do they just get thrown away? I'm going find out. And if they do count, I think I just found myself a new strategy.

Raquel Z. Rivera *is an author, professor, and freelance journalist from San Juan, Puerto Rico.*

The sistahs of the Hip-Hop generation will soon be acknowledged to be the true leaders of our communities. Not just symbolically speaking, but in all of its social, political, material, and spiritual manifestations. It our time to step, to be heard, and to lead!
—Zenzele Isoke, Hip-Hop activist

P-Diddy tells folks to Vote or Die!
People are dying—in the ghetto, in Iraq, in Sudan, on the Mexican border.
I voted. They're still dying. Did I miss something, Mr. Diddy?
—Julia Ahumada Grob, *Revolutions in Hip-Hop*

I Don't Vote

by Manuela Arciniegas

I don't vote.

Don't vote for no dream-breaking, disappointing, too-brown-to-be-white dope.

The Bronx is swarmed with dirty politicians.

Helping out a young Boricua man in 1998 who ran a campaign against twenty-year incumbent assemblywoman Gloria Davis had the granny trying to spank us for "misbehaving" by trying to steal her cushy job. She threw the muscle of the Bronx political machine at us, and had me wondering, Where is the democracy? Granny snatched flyers out of our hands so fast I thought she was running for a check! She even cursed at the folks sitting on Bronx park benches for responding to our positive messages and a little hope. She just got busted and fired for pocketing money from Bronx government construction deals. She was also the only black woman I saw holding office in the South Bronx.

I found out that Waste Management, the biggest waste-handling company in this *cabron* world, was funding my borough president. When that same president went down to get arrested in Vieques but wouldn't bat an eyelash at Hunts Point's whispers against the asthma choking all of us (it could of been screams, but asthma gets in the way of us being loud, you know), I fell off my democracy-loving cloud and turned my back on institutionalized government.

When Bill Clinton called me "girl" for delivering a box of peaches to his office, I thought, fuck a White House internship, white man is running this ship, I'm here to kiss ass, tame my 'fro, and go with this flow? Outta here.

The one time I went to try to vote, listening to that voice that blares, "Do what you're told," I walked across the street from my project building into another project building where the booths were. I waited as Doña somebody looked down on me and up her book for my name for a good fifteen minutes until she finally told me, "Your polling place is four blocks away in P.S. Oogeleboogele." I told her, "Don't you see it's pouring outside? I live less than twenty paces away from this building!" She told me, "I'm just doing my job. You can't vote here."

What I heard was, "You can't vote. Don't even try it. And if you do, it ain't gonna make a difference anyway."

Mierda. Cabron.

That's why I don't vote.

Yet.

Manuela Arciniegas *is a cultural arts educator and administrator. Manuela believes in advancing African diaspora cultural arts for the empowerment of communities.*

You are so fired, Mr. Sick Son of a Bitch; open your eyes and take a look.
—Lily Nolte, ranter

Every Breath Counts
by Marinieves Alba

For indigenous lands and people, across the world.
For the people of the occupied territories, from Palestine to Boriken

nation restrained by barbed-wire fences
poisonous seeds of greed
spawn dehumanization
whispers of freedom carried on desert winds
like drops of life
an oasis
visions of liberation
no to foreign occupation!
vivid and dreamlike palette of freedom
red, white, and blue
hues of lifeless color
dripping off the bodies of fallen soldiers
streaming down the faces of prayerful mothers
kneeling beneath crying skies
lost souls wander
voices carried on howling winds
rays of light mark the path of ancestors
new breaths signal
freedom within

BREATHE IN . . . BREATHE OUT!

Marinieves Alba is a twenty-nine-year-old Puerto Rican and Panamanian activist, educator, writer, and media professional from the South Bronx.

I Vote Every Time I Get the Chance

by Shaquesha Alequin

I vote every time I get the chance
But this ain't about me
I wanna talk about marching protesting poster-making registered voters
    that don't vote
I wanna talk about MTV Rock the Vote parties that target young black
    men and tell them that if they want change . . . their vote counts
Chalk that bullshit up with the lies my teacher told me, the lies my
    preacher told me,
      the lies my people told me:
      Vote Democratic 'cuz Republicans don't care about colored folks
But in my 'hood, colored folks don't care about colored folks
They got us believing that the only way out of the 'hood is
    Sports, drugs, or entertainment
And they still want me to congregate around my brothers and tell
    them some shit I know
    I don't believe?
Tell them "dog, dog, dog, for real, yo, our vote matters, yo!"
But tell a black man in Florida that his vote counted and see how
    long it takes
    for the spit to run down your cheek

I wanna talk about the celebrity-endorsed commercials that think
    they can get the young folks to vote 'cuz of their popularity status.

{ **263** }

We ain't stupid enough to pay full price for your wack-ass album and you expect us to fall for that shit?

I wanna talk about ten-minute visits thru people-of-color 'hoods in rented vans blasting slogans and stapling Kinko's-printed vote-for-me posters of politicians that say they're from our community, when the grandmas that have been in this 'hood for forty-plus years do not know their face.

I don't wanna talk about politicians who rape states for votes to steal elections and sacrifice thousands of lives to build up the economy and write themselves a check for 87 billion pieces of green paper so they can wipe their crooked-ass cracks with it 'cuz the paper's a little softer, after my folks done sweated so hard for it.

Yet, I vote
Every day
In every prayer, in every chant, and these ballots don't get cast
    'cuz there is no box to check for their freedom
For love
For truth
For knowledge
For life
For peace

Shaquesha Alequin, *born and raised in the South Bronx, is a multitalented Afro-Borinquen artist of many mediums. She uses all that she knows about her heritage in her expressions and is launching a clothing line and releasing a book of her writing in 2006. She has been a member of the organizing and activism community since age fifteen and currently works facilitating an after-school program in Harlem.*

I Will Vote

by Anna Lappé and Sara Littlecrow Russell
from the We Got Issues! Performance Piece

I guess voting is casting my vote, only it never seems to matter; my candidates never win. So, instead, unplugging my TV is casting my vote.

I will vote the day a candidate goes to the Wounded Knee Memorial, slashes his arms in grief, and gets down on his knees to beg for forgiveness for the slaughter of 267 unarmed Lakota refugees.

Canceling my newspaper subscriptions for biased coverage is casting my vote.

I will vote the day after a presidential candidate walks into the board room of a Fortune 500 company and demands 385 years of lost wages to be returned to the descendents of slaves.

Choosing to do work I believe in (and not making much money) is casting my vote.

I will vote the day after a presidential candidate spends a day picking pesticide-encrusted vegetables in a blazing California field.

Buying fair trade coffee and family farm–raised food is casting my vote.

I will vote the day a candidate speaks to me in Spanish or Mandarin or Portuguese or Khmer or Urdu or even Swahili—anything but English!

I will vote the day a candidate spends a January night in a cardboard box in the park.

I will vote the day a candidate makes his elite Yale fraternity giveback Geronimo's skull.

Cutting up my Citibank card is casting my vote.

I will vote the day a candidate showers in Agent Orange before telling me it's safe.

Dating a woman is casting my vote. Dating a man and being his equal is casting my vote.

I will vote the day a candidate escorts a pregnant woman through a screaming mob to get her safely into an abortion clinic.

Loving my grandmother's memories is casting my vote. Protesting against police brutality is casting my vote.

I will vote the day a candidate's child is arrested under the Patriot Act.

Calling my congressman is casting my vote. And yet I still vote, because I have to believe that voting is casting my vote even though I am still not convinced it makes a difference. It's just too depressing to think that I may never make one at all.

Anna Lappé *and* **Sara Littlecrow Russell**'s *voting rant is part of the WGI! Performance Piece.*

Ritual of Empowerment

A New Pledge of Allegiance

This may seem radical to some of you, but for those who have not felt very inspired by our country lately, this ritual could be just the ticket.

The Pledge of Allegiance was written in 1892 and reflected the specific concerns of the founding fathers and their subsequent lineage. Give yourself the task of redrafting this pledge and making it relevant to *your* passions, issues, and concerns.

Using a large sheet of drawing paper, markers, and crayons, create your own personal flag that will serve as a backdrop for your own personal pledge of allegiance. Find a space where you can hang your flag and recite your new pledge.

Make a commitment to recite your new pledge (new or the original if you are reclaiming it) every day for the next thirty days; during that time, contemplate all the ways in which you contribute to making this nation a true democracy. Make a commitment to do one new thing this year to celebrate your pledge and the vision that this great nation was founded on.

We Got Stats!

➡️ In 2003, **8.3% of employed immigrant workers were business owners**, as compared with 6.2% of native-born women.
—Susan Pearce. Immigration Policy in Focus, Volume 4, Issue 1 (2005)

➡️ Since the 1984 elections, **women's voting rates have continued to surpass that of men's.** —U.S. Census Bureau (2000)

➡️ **Never married, widowed, and divorced women** make up 46% of all women and 24% of the eligible voting population, but they register and **vote at a markedly lower rate** than their married counterparts. —Gayle White. *Atlanta Journal Constitution* (2004)

➡️ **Undocumented women have lower participation (62%) in the labor force** than undocumented men or U.S.–born women. —Jeffrey Passel, Randolph Capps, and Michael Fix. Urban Institute (2004)

➡️ The Violence Against Women Act, which was enacted in 1994, entitles undocumented women and their children to a **speedy citizenship process if they are being abused.**
—Robert Reeves and Elsie Hui Arias. *Las Vegas Asian Journal* (2005)

➡️ **Voting among those age 18 to 29** jumped sharply from 40% to 49% from 2000 to the 2004 elections, **though it was still lower than its 1972 high** of 55%.
—The Center for Information & Research on Civic Learning and Engagement (2004)

➤

➡️ **Young women are more likely to vote than men,**
with 52% of women between 18 and 24, voting in the 2004
election, compared to only 45% of men the same age.
—The Center for Information & Research on Civic Learning and Engagement (2004)

➡️ A recent survey found that **most women between 18
and 24** feel that going into politics would force them to
compromise their beliefs, and that, ultimately,
direct service is the best way to make an impact.
—The White House Project

➡️ Though more than 1 million households are headed by women
age 15 to 24, and these young women are more likely than men
to work and pay taxes, **government spending—such as
the current focus on abstinence-education programs—does not adequately address young
women's needs.** —The National Center for Research on Women (2004)

➡️ Each year, **8,000 to 12,000 U.S. men find foreign
wives or "mail-order brides"** through for-profit
brokers. In 2005, Congress passed a law that would enable
these women to receive criminal information on their
potential husbands before entering the United States.
—Jim Haley. Herald Net (2005)

Transmogrified Visions
by Hilda Herrera
from the We Got Issues! Performance Piece

I dreamed of women in white cotton garments lined along the banks of an
unknown river.
The sun gleamed against their skin causing their hardships to perspire.
Like rain, the drops of their salted sweat blended with the river
waters.
The click-clack of stones against the fabric they were washing
resonated through the atmosphere like the hands of old souls beating on
drums. Their bodies moved in choreographed motions, dancing in unison
to the rhythm of their daily chores.

Suddenly, the women in white cotton garments shifted to images of women
adorned with kaleidoscopes of colorful dashikis. The hands of those old
souls were no longer beating on drums, but were fisted on the combs
that picked each strand of hair in their afros.
And there were long-haired, white-skinned women wearing bell-bottom
jeans, caressing the strands of guitars as they san songs of freedom.
The loudness of their voices pierced through segregation, erasing
invisible barriers, as they stood together in sisterhood. The picket
signs in their hands spoke through red ink verbalizing their demands:

"EQUALITY! EDUCATION! BETTER JOBS! BETTER PAY! NO WAR!
"EQUALITY! EDUCATION! BETTER JOBS! BETTER PAY! NO WAR!
"EQUALITY! EDUCATION! BETTER JOBS! BETTER PAY! NO WAR!
"EQUALITY! EDUCATION! BETTER JOBS! BETTER PAY! NO WAR!

I was enjoying this dream so much, I didn't want it to end.

Acknowledgments

Our mentors and supporters: Elizabeth Lesser, Gail Straub, David Gershon, Jodie Evans, Eve Ensler, Jane Fonda, Allison Prouty, Jerrilynn Fields, Nina Simons, Stephen Reichtschaffen, Claudine Brown, Karen Garrett, Grant Garrison, Ben Rodriguez Cubeñas, Hugh Hogan, Caron Atlas, Coleen Trimble, Amy Pilling, Wendy Flick, and Chris Mednick.

Funders of WGI: V-Day, The North Star Fund, Nathan Cummings Foundation, The Rockefeller Brothers Fund, The Pond Foundation, and The Collective Heritage Institute. Our Collaborators in this work: The Empowerment Institute, Center for Civic Participation, Codepink, The League of Young Voters, Code Pink, The Prison Moratorium Project, Omega Institute, Bioneers, and many, many others. Our wonderful individual donors are way too many to name!

Our partners in this work: Colorado Hip-Hop Association, Denver Pan African Arts Society, Santa Fe Art Institute, Tewa Women United/V Keepers, EarthCare Institute, Intermedia Arts, Minneapolis YWCA, The Loft/Equilibrium, University of Minnesota Women's Studies Department, New Mexico Community Foundation.

WGI staff, board members, and interns, past and present! Especially: Rebecca Lynn Wilson, Tamila Woodard, Christine Murray, Michelle Lucien, Onome Djere, Julia A. Grob, Alli Maxwell, Ninoska Deoleo, Jessica Roman, Piper Anderson, Aleeka Wade, Manuela Arciniegas, Lenora Pace, and Julie Kline. Interns: Rosa Cohen-Cruz, Shanna Bowie, Heather Wallerson, Kim Howard, Yasmine Bluma Lancaster, and Jewell Lourdes Mercer.

Our beloved writers: Sara Littlecrow Russell, Lenelle Möise, Hilda Herrera, Anna Lappé, and Stacey Ann Chin.

Special thanks to those women featured in our book, and of course, to all of our courageous RANTERS!

To our amazing participants in the first class of the WGI Leadership Development Institute for Young Women: Adeeba Rana, Allison Joy Faelner, Marla Teyolia, Kamilah Forbes, Kelly Tsai, Jennifer Cendaña Armas, Fly Yvonne O. Etaghene, and Chelsea Michel Gregory.

Our agent, Jennifer Cayea; our publisher, Karen Bouris; Ani Chamichian, Alma Bune, and all the diva staff at Inner Ocean Publishing.

Rha Goddess would like to thank: My wonderful husband, partner, and best friend, Corey Kupfer, my father, Fred Sr., my sisters, Kimberly and Michelle, my niece, Nieta, my nephew, Freddie III, my loving in-laws, Cecille and Howard, and the rest of the Kupfer-O'Leary Clan. My personal mentors, Sheree Stomberg, Tad Motyka, Charlee Sutton, Rosemary Blake. My partners in life and liberation, Daniel and Adam, Kate, Billy, Clyde, Ghana and Will, Brookie and Lee, and Byron. My theatrical agents, Cathy Zimmerman, Ann Rosenthal, and the awesome staff at MAPP; my Zulu fam; my ESR fam; and my IBS fam.

    Special Thanks: Mildred, Steve, Chay, Rennie, Will P., Darrin, Sarah G., Craig, Emi, Djibril, Anisa, Nikki, Ramsey, Andy, Lenora, Maurine, Sekou, Roberta, Wesley, Andrea, Genny, Tracey, Anna, Talvin, Marc M., Merv A., Peter F., Yvonne B., Baraka, Marty, Mark R., Suzanne, Karen S., Sandy A, Stacy P., BoaPhi, Rachel B., and all of the amazing artists, activists, and revolutionaries I have had the privilege of working with.

JLove Calderón would like to thank: A very special shout-out to my amazing husband, Hector, and sons, Gabriel Amani and Camilo Mandela; you three have taught me how to love completely. To my family: my mom, Anne, and her partner, Rick; my dad, Peter; my brothers, John and Peter; and my sister-in-law, Shannon. To Hector's family: Hector Sr., Nina, José, Carmen, Alma, Ana Lucia, and Quico. My Denver, Cincinnati, and Indiana relatives, and my entire El Puente Fam! And, of course, the R.E.A.C.Hip-Hop crew! All my Hip-Hop activist homies from the Cali to New York and everywhere in between!

    Thank you for being my lifeline, my sanity: Asia, Joanna, Lalania, Vania, Anda, Marti, Kim, Brandy, Wanda, Julia, Alli, Angela, Teresa, Aroosha, Rosa, Rafael, Beth, Todd, Sam, Damien, Dennis, Cathy W., Sofia, Fidel, Kuttin' Kandi, Eli Ceballos, and all the folks in the trenches working collectively to fight for truth, freedom, and justice.

And to our collective fam: Danny H., Suheir H., Daphne F., Baba, and April S.

About the Editors

Eli Ceballos

JLove Calderón is an author, educator, and activist who's been working with young people from California to New York for the past fifteen years. She's a cofounder of the legendary B-Boy Summit, and worked for eleven years at the first ever Hip-Hop and human rights public school, the El Puente Academy for Peace and Justice in Brooklyn. JLove's been published in the *Source, Clamor,* and the *Ave,* as well as featured in the *New York Times, Self* magazine, the *Source, Punk Planet,* and on the *Oprah Winfrey Show*. Her debut novel, *White Girl* (Atria/Simon & Schuster), is due out in 2007, and she's coediting *Till the White Day Is Done,* a book about white privilege, Hip-Hop, and social change. Check out www.jlovecalderon.com for more information about her upcoming projects.

Rha Goddess is a performing artist and social/political activist. Her work has been internationally featured in several compilations, anthologies, forums, and festivals. As founder and CEO of Divine Dime Entertainment, Ltd., she was one of the first women in Hip-Hop to independently market and commercially distribute her own music worldwide. In May 2000, *Essence* magazine recognized Rha as one of its "30 Women to Watch." In 2002, BAM's prestigious Next Wave/NextNext festival chose her as one of six artists deemed to be influential in the next decade. Her activist work includes cofounding the Sista II Sista Freedom School for Young Women of Color and being the former International Spokeswoman for the Universal Zulu Nation. Visit Rha at www.rhaworld.com.

About We Got Issues!

When I care to be powerful—to use my strength in the service of my vision, then it becomes less and less important whether I am afraid.

—Audre Lourde

Yes! I want to support powerful women!

RANT!

Raise your voice and speak your mind! Release your passions, ideas, feelings, and fears. Read your rant to five friends, enter it in our hottest rant section, and if you win, we will post it on our website for the world to read! Log on: http://www.wegotissues.org/rant

DONATE!

Give money! Support your local women-centered nonprofits. Every little bit counts. You can also support We Got Issues! Leadership Institute for Young Women, and our National Tour. Log on: http://www.wegotissues.org/5Drive or make checks payable to 1+1+1=ONE. *Coming Soon:* WGI!'s new Financial Empowerment Initiative: Put Your Money Where Your Heart Is!

CONNECT!

If you are in the New York area, join us! Become an Institute Participant, volunteer, or intern. Sign up for the WGI! Newsletter. Stay connected with the organizations in our resource guide. E-mail us at: wegotissues@gmail.com

Send Mail to:
We Got Issues!
c/o 1+1+1=ONE
190 N 10th Street Suite 303
Brooklyn, NY 11211
E-mail: wegotissues@gmail.com
Website: www.wegotissues.org